I0013445

Real-World STEM Tutorial & Software

Science, Technology, Engineering and Math Problems

3rd Edition

By
Philip Conrod & Lou Tylee

© 2019 Kidware Software LLC

PO Box 701
Maple Valley, WA 98038
http://www.kidwaresoftware.com

Copyright © 2019 by Kidware Software LLC.   All rights reserved

Kidware Software LLC
PO Box 701
Maple Valley, Washington 98038
1.425.413.1185
www.kidwaresoftware.com

All Rights Reserved. No part of the contents of this book may be reproduced or transmitted in any form or by any means without the written permission of the publisher.

Printed in the United States of America

ISBN-13: 978-1-951077-30-3 (Printed Edition)
ISBN-13: 978-1-951077-31-0 (Electronic Edition)

Cover Design and Illustation by Anton Khrupin
Additional Illustrations by Anton Khrupin, Leyn, Who_I_Am & Igor Korchak

This copy of the "Real-World STEM" and the associated software is licensed to a single user. Multiple copy licenses are available for educational institutions. Please contact Kidware Software for school site license information. Copies of the course are not to be distributed or provided to any other user.

This textbook was developed for the course, "Real-World STEM", produced by Kidware Software, Maple Valley, Washington. The 3rd Edition does not include any software and only displays screenshots from our commercial STEM software. We have included screenshots from our Windows Version 8 STEM Simulation software for illustration purposes only. Our STEM software can be licensed separately by contacting Kidware Software and the software is only compatible with Microsoft Windows version 8 and older Operating Systems.   The STEM demonstration is NOT compatible with Microsoft Windows 10.

This guide refers to several software and hardware products by their trade names. These references are for informational purposes only and all trademarks are the property of their respective companies and owners.   Microsoft, Visual Studio, Visual Basic, Visual C#, IntelliSense, Word, Excel, MSDN, and Windows are all trademark products of the Microsoft Corporation.

The example companies, organizations, products, domain names, e-mail addresses, logos, people, places, and events depicted are fictitious. No association with any real company, organization, product, domain name, e-mail address, logo, person, place, or event is intended or should be inferred.

This book expresses the author's views and opinions. The information in this book is distributed on an "as is" basis, without and expresses, statutory, or implied warranties.

Neither the author(s) nor Kidware Software LLC shall have any liability to any person or entity with respect to any loss nor damage caused or alleged to be caused directly or indirectly by the information contained in this book.

About the Authors

Philip Conrod has authored, co-authored and edited over two dozen computer programming books over the past thirty years. Philip holds a bachelor's degree in Computer Information Systems and a Master's certificate in the Essentials of Business Development from Regis University. Philip has served in various Information Technology leadership roles in companies like Sundstrand Aerospace, Safeco Insurance, FamilyLife, Kenworth Truck Company, PACCAR Inc, and Darigold Inc. Today, Philip serves as the President & Publisher of Kidware Software LLC. Philip and his family live in Maple Valley, Washington.

Lou Tylee holds BS and MS degrees in Mechanical Engineering and a PhD in Electrical Engineering. Lou has been programming computers since 1969 when he took his first Fortran course in college. He has written software to control suspensions for high speed ground vehicles, monitor nuclear power plants, lower noise levels in commercial jetliners, compute takeoff speeds for jetliners, locate and identify air and ground traffic and to let kids count bunnies, learn how to spell and do math problems. He has written several on-line texts teaching Visual Basic, Visual C# and Java to thousands of people. He taught computer programming courses for over 15 years at the University of Washington and currently teaches math and engineering courses at the Oregon Institute of Technology. Lou also works as a research engineer at a major Seattle aerospace firm. He is the proud father of five children, has six grandchildren and is married to an amazing woman. Lou and his family live in Seattle, Washington.

Acknowledgements

I want to thank my three wonderful daughters - Stephanie, Jessica and Chloe, who helped with various aspects of the book publishing process including software testing, book editing, creative design and many other more tedious tasks like finding errors and typos. I could not have accomplished this without all your hard work, love and support. I want to also thank my best friend Jesus, who has always been there by my side giving me wisdom and guidance. Without you, this textbook would have never been printed or published.

I also want to thank my multi-talented co-author, Lou Tylee, for doing all the real hard work necessary to develop, test, debug, and keep current all the applications, games and base tutorial text found in this book. Lou has tirelessly poured his heart and soul into so many previous versions of this tutorial and there are so many beginners who have benefited from his work over the years. Lou is by far one of the best application developers and tutorial writers I have ever worked with. Thank you, Lou, for collaborating with me on this book project.

Table of Contents

1. Problem Solving

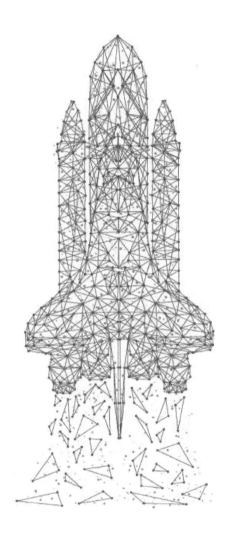

Introduction

The typical classroom textbook problem involves presentation of some pertinent facts and asks for a particular piece of information. The students use whatever they have learned up to that point in their STEM education to develop the problem and solve it. These are valuable exercises, but they do not address the full spectrum of what is required to solve a real problem. Let's look at some of the steps in solving real problems. The steps presented here apply to problem solving in general and not just the example problem we'll look at next.

A good approach to solving real problems is to ask the following questions (these are used in solving the example problem):

1. What are we trying to find out?
2. What information is available?
3. What information is pertinent?
4. What is the problem we need to solve?
5. Can we solve the problem?
6. If we can solve it, how do we solve it?
7. Does the solution we obtain make sense? Is it acceptable?
8. Is there more than one solution? If so, which is the best?
9. When are we done solving the problem?

Let's look at each of these questions and discuss their implications.

First, we need to know what we are trying to find. This is sometimes fairly simple, but many times a very involved process. The important thing is to be able to write down what we are looking for. Next, we gather all information needed to solve the problem. It's best to gather too much information than too little. But, a good problem solver can quickly see what information is pertinent and what is not. Once we have written down what we think the problem is, the mathematics of problem solving come into play.

A big step in solving real problems is deciding how to solve the problem. Or, deciding we can't solve the problem. If we decide the problem is not solvable, we either have to give up (not a good option) or rewrite the problem so it is solvable. In the classroom, the solution approach is usually dictated by the topic currently being covered. That is, if you've just spent the last couple of days discussing multiplication, you can bet your homework problems probably require the use of multiplication. We can't do that in solving real problems. The solver must decide what tool in his/her mathematical toolbox is the best.

So now, we have our problem and we know how we're going to try to solve it. We apply the selected techniques and come up with an answer. How do we know our answer is correct? Well first, we must carefully check all operations to make sure the mathematics were applied correctly and consistently. The answer can't be correct if the math was done wrong. If possible, substitute the solution back in the original equations and check for correctness. And, the best check on a problem's solution is its physical reasonableness. The answer must make sense! For example, if we're solving a problem that requires a car speed and the answer comes out negative or 500 miles per hour, we should have some clue something has gone wrong somewhere. If the answer doesn't make sense, we need to find out why. Was the problem written incorrectly? Was it posed incorrectly? Was the math done correctly? We need to constantly check ourselves during the problem-solving process to make sure proper and correct approaches are followed. I personally feel this idea of checking for the reasonableness of an answer is one of the most important aspects of problem solving.

Assume we have solved our problem and the answer makes sense. The next question is; is the answer adequate? Many times, after we meticulously apply the math to our stated problem to get a correct answer, the answer is not acceptable. Perhaps it doesn't meet some cost guidelines or performance requirements. What do we do then? We have to change something in our problem formulation - add/delete information until the answer we obtain is a correct and acceptable solution. But then we need to ask: is this the only correct and acceptable solution? Many real problems have multiple solutions. It is then the problem solver's job to decide which solution is the best. What criteria are applied to decide which is "best?" Criteria such as cost, dependability, time of production, resource consumption, and other measures of goodness must be developed to make such a decision.

So now, assume we have solved our posed problem and found the best, correct, acceptable solution. Are we done? This is a very difficult question to answer.

Since we started out not knowing what the problem was, how we were going to solve it, or what the correct answer was, it's quite hard to determine when you are done. The key element to making this decision is judgment. If your judgment (which obviously is a very subjective concept) tells you that you are done, then you probably are done. But if, in subsequent work with this problem, you decide the solution was not acceptable, you must return to the problem and make the necessary changes to obtain an acceptable solution.

This last question, that being if you are done, points out an important part of the problem-solving process. It is iterative. If, at some point in the solution process, something doesn't work or doesn't make sense, you must return to a previous step and do whatever is necessary to reformulate the problem or solution to correct the error(s). This may be something as simple as correcting a math error or something as involved as completely starting over. And, unfortunately, in the real-world of problem solving you can't just give up and wait to see how the teacher solved the problem.

Now, let's look at several real-world STEM (Science, Technology, Engineering and Math) problems.

2. Home Heating Mathematics

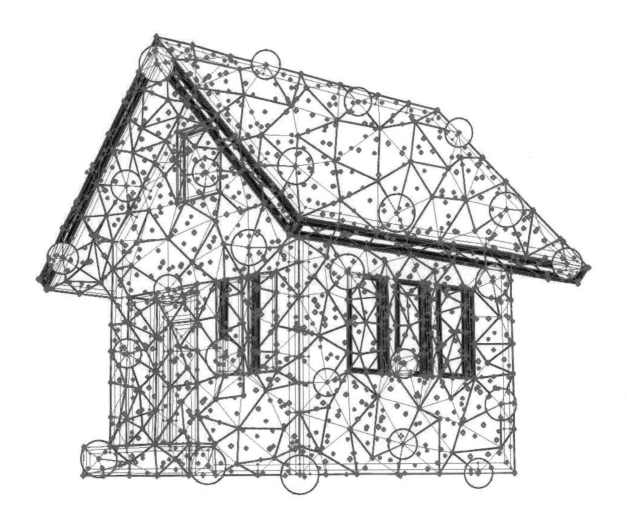

Introduction

This chapter provides an application of a real-world math problem in one particular area, that of home heating. We discuss the mathematics behind a thermostat and provide equations that allow computation of temperature changes within a home. Sample problems are given, as well as suggestions for further study.

What a Thermostat Does

By itself, the furnace in your home is not a very practical device. It has only two possible states, on or off, neither of which results in a desirable condition. If it was on all the time, your house would be very warm and your wallet very empty. If it was off all the time, your house would be very cold and your pipes very frozen (in the winter months at least). The thermostat's job is then to turn the furnace on and off to meet some desired performance. We say the thermostat provides control for the furnace.

Figure 1 shows how the thermostat controls the furnace in your home heating system.

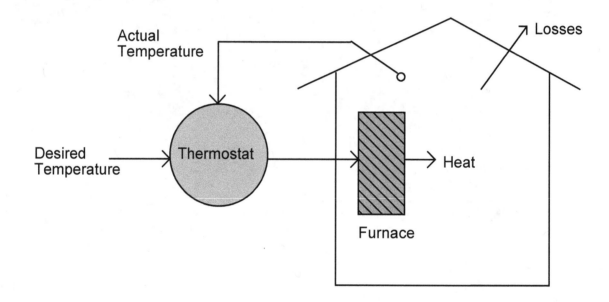

Figure 1. Home heating system

The desired temperature ($T_{desired}$ - you set this on your thermostat) is compared to the actual temperature (T_{actual} - measured within the thermostat) and the temperature difference used by the thermostat to determine whether or not to turn on the furnace. The furnace (if on) delivers hot air to the home, increasing air temperature. If the furnace is off, losses through the walls and windows decrease the air temperature. A law for turning the furnace on and off is needed.

One possible "control law" for the furnace would be

$$T_{desired} - T_{actual} > 0, \text{ Turn furnace on}$$
$$T_{desired} - T_{actual} < 0, \text{ Turn furnace off}$$

Immediately, we see a problem with this law. The moment the actual temperature drops below the desired temperature, the furnace will turn on. The air will heat up and the actual temperature will rise above the desired temperature, causing a quick shutdown of the furnace. Hence, the furnace would be constantly turning on and off, causing great wear and tear. A better law, and the one used by household thermostats is

$$T_{desired} - T_{actual} > e, \text{ Turn furnace on}$$
$$T_{desired} - T_{actual} < e, \text{ Turn furnace off}$$
$$-e < T_{desired} - T_{actual} < e, \text{ Leave furnace in current state (on or off)}$$

where e is some positive number. This control law is sketched in Figure 2.

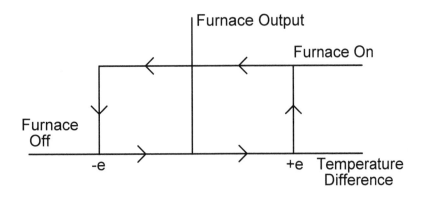

Figure 2. Furnace control law

This new law just says if the desired temperature and actual temperature are within e degrees of each other, don't change anything. Otherwise, either turn on or turn off the furnace. Note if e is too small, the above-mentioned cycling problem is encountered. If e is too large, your house would go through large temperature swings. Usually, e is about 2 degrees.

Heating Your Home

We've looked at a description of thermostat performance. Now, let's look at a description of how the furnace and heating/cooling of the house perform. These equations (or one's like them) can be used to "size" a furnace for a certain home, determine how good a job home insulation is doing, or do an economic analysis on the benefits of installing more insulation. Similar equations are used in determining cooling requirements for jet engines, automobile engines, and spacecraft surfaces.

It's pretty simple to describe the furnace performance, it's either putting out heat or it's not:

$$\text{Furnace Output} = Q = Q_{max} \text{ (Btu/hr), if on}$$
$$= 0 \text{ (Btu/hr), if off}$$

where Q_{max} is maximum furnace output. A Btu (British thermal unit) is a measure of energy.

The house heating/cooling dynamics are described by doing a heat balance on the home, that is, determining all sources of heat gain, heat loss, and heat storage. The basic balance equation is

$$\text{Heat Stored} = \text{Heat Gained} - \text{Heat Lost}$$

Heat gained is simply the furnace output (we'll ignore any solar heat gained through windows). Heat is lost through the exterior surfaces of your home and is described by

$$\text{Heat Lost} = A(T_h - T_o)/R$$

In this equation, A is the exterior area of all walls, windows, and ceilings of your home that face outside, T_h is the air temperature in your home, T_o is the outside air temperature, and R is the so-called 'R factor' always advertised (the Pink Panther commercials) as a measure of insulation effectiveness. Notice the larger the R factor is, the less heat will be lost from your home. Finally, the heat stored is

$$\text{Heat Stored} = C\Delta T_h/\Delta t$$

where C is heat capacity, a measure of how fast the air in your home can be heated, and ΔT_h is how much the temperature in your house changes over the time period Δt. Substituting these relations into the heat balance equation yields:

$$C\Delta T_h/\Delta t = Q - A(T_h - T_o)/R$$

With these equations, we can do some fairly interesting computations. First, we'll need some typical numbers to plug in. The heat capacity is a product of the mass of air in your home and a quantity known as specific heat. The specific heat of air at room temperature is

$$\text{Specific Heat} = 0.24 \text{ Btu/lb-}°F$$

To compute the mass of air, we need to know the house dimensions. Assume we have a house 45 feet by 45 feet (a square house?), hence a floor area of 2025 square feet. With 8-foot ceilings, the total air volume is 16,200 cubic feet. Air density is approximately 0.075 pounds per cubic foot, so the mass of air in a typical home is

$$\text{Mass of Air} = (16{,}200 \text{ ft}^3)(0.075 \text{ lb/ft}^3) = 1215 \text{ lb}$$

That's over half a ton of air! Then, the heat capacity of that air is

$$C = \text{Heat Capacity} = \text{Mass x Specific Heat} = (1215 \text{ lb})(0.24 \text{ Btu/lb-}°\text{F}) = 2916 \text{ Btu/}°\text{F}$$

The exterior surface area includes the four perimeter walls and the ceiling

$$A = \text{Exterior Area} = 4(45 \text{ ft x 8 ft}) + 2025 \text{ ft}^2 = 3465 \text{ ft}^2$$

The last two pieces of information we need are furnace output and an R factor. A typical furnace has an output of 100,000 Btu/hr, so

$$Q = 100{,}000 \text{ Btu/hr (if furnace on)}$$
$$= 0 \text{ (if furnace off)}$$

We will assume a windowless house and assume that the heat lost through the perimeter walls is the same as through the ceiling. We make these assumptions so we can use a single R factor. Obviously, windows have a lower R factor than walls - we could account for this fact with just a little more algebra. For example, if we wanted to separate wall and window losses, the heat loss equation would be

$$\text{Heat Loss} = A_{window}(T_h - T_o)/R_{window} + A_{wall}(T_h - T_o)/R_{wall}$$

where A_{window} is the total window surface area and R_{window} is the corresponding R factor for the windows. Similarly, A_{wall} is wall surface area and R_{wall} is the wall R factor. And, maybe not so obviously, more heat is lost through the ceiling than the walls of a house. As we all know, heat rises, hence the air at the ceiling is hotter than the heat on the floor. And we see in the heat loss equation, that the hotter the house air is, the more heat is lost. That's why we put more insulation in ceilings than in walls. But, for this work, we assume that the air temperature is the same no matter where we measure it in the house.

So, only considering wall losses, the R factor is computed using

$$R = h/k$$

where h is the insulation thickness and k is thermal conductivity, a measure of how well a substance conducts heat. Obviously, we want high thickness and low thermal conductivity for a good insulator. But high thickness means high cost in thicker walls during construction and more insulation. We must make some compromises based on cost analyses. Here, assume we are using three inches of fiberglass (which has a k = 0.0239 Btu/hr-ft-°F), or the R factor is:

$$R = h/k = (0.25 \text{ ft})/(0.0239 \text{ Btu/hr-ft-°F}) = 10.5 \text{ hr-ft}^2\text{-°F/Btu}$$

With all these numbers, we can now solve some typical problems. Recall the heat balance equation is

$$C\Delta T_h/\Delta t = Q - A(T_h - T_o)/R$$

or with the numbers substituted

$$(2916)\Delta T_h/\Delta t = Q - 3465(T_h - T_o)/10.5$$

In this equation, the temperatures are in °F, the furnace output in Btu/hr (either Q = 100,000 if on or 0 if off), and the time is in hours.

Problem 1: You've just come home. It's 30°F (T_o) outside and 60°F (T_h) in your house. How long will it take to heat it up to 70°F?

When you turn the thermostat up to 70°F ($T_{desired}$), the furnace will come on, so its output is 100,000 Btu/hr, and we want a ΔT_h of 10°F (70 - 60). First, solving for Δt

$$\Delta t = (2916)\Delta T_h/[Q - 3465(T_h - T_o)/10.5]$$

and now substituting the numbers

$$\Delta t = (2916)(10)/[100,000 - 3465(60 - 30)/10.5] = 0.324 \text{ hr} = 19.4 \text{ minutes}$$

Notice this answer isn't exactly right because we leave T_h at 60 degrees even though the house is heating up. But during heating, the furnace output is much larger than the heat losses, so the approximation is actually quite good.

Problem 2: It's February and 10°F outside (T_o). You've left for the day ($\Delta t = 8$ hours) and mistakenly left your thermostat so low, the furnace will never turn on. When you left, it was 70°F in your house (T_h). Will your pipes begin to freeze?

Let's see how cold it will get in your house. Here, the furnace is off so its output is zero. The heat balance equation tells us the temperature drop will be

$$\Delta T_h = -(3465)(T_h - T_o)(\Delta t)/(10.5)(2916)$$
$$= -(3465)(70 - 10)(8)/(10.5)(2916) = -54.3°F$$

So, the equation says when you get home the temperature in your house will be 70 - 54.3 or, 15.7°F. Should you start thawing out pipes and call a plumber? Don't panic! Remember in the last problem we could ignore the fact the house temperature was changing in computing heat gain, because the furnace output was much greater than the losses? Well, here we can't ignore that change, because heat loss is all we are dealing with. That is, note we left T_h at 70°F to compute the losses even though we know that temperature is decreasing with time, which decreases the losses. Hence, our model is not adequate for computing temperature changes when the furnace is not on (actually it's sufficient as long as the furnace is not off too long).

To exactly determine the temperature change in this problem requires the use of exponentials. The exact temperature change, with the furnace off, is (don't worry where this comes from)

$$\Delta T_h = (T_h - T_o)[e^{-(3465)(\Delta t)/(10.5)(2916)} - 1]$$

where e is a constant approximately equal to 2.718281828. With our numbers (T_h = 70°F, T_o = 10°F, Δt = 8 hours), we find the house temperature drops 35.7°F, making the temperature when you get home 34.3°F, still cold, but your pipes should be safe.

We can approximate the result obtained from this exact solution by using the simpler equation

$$\Delta T_h = -(3465)(T_h - 10)(\Delta t)/(10.5)(2916)$$

over a shorter period of time and after computing the temperature loss for that period, substitute the resulting T_h back into the equation to determine the heat loss over the next period of time. Let's let that time period be one hour (Δt = 1) and compute temperature drops for 8 hours. This results in a computation table like

19

Time (hr)	T_h (°F) at start	ΔT_h (°F)	T_h (°F) at end
0-1	70.0	-6.8	63.2
1-2	63.2	-6.0	57.2
2-3	57.2	-5.4	51.8
3-4	51.8	-4.7	47.1
4-5	47.1	-4.2	42.9
5-6	42.9	-3.7	39.2
6-7	39.2	-3.3	35.9
7-8	35.9	-2.9	33.0

The final result of 33.0°F compares favorably with the exact answer (34.3°F). Closer agreement would be obtained with finer time change increments. For example, if the computation were done every six minutes ($\Delta t = 0.1$ hours), we get a final answer of 34.1°F.

This last case points out a consideration that must be made when solving problems. The problem solver must be aware of under what conditions the mathematics (the furnace/heating model here) being used are adequate. And when inadequate, what changes must be made to solve the problem? We saw that our simple model was OK when the furnace was on, but not when it was left off for any significant amount of time. Hence, we had to develop the more complicated exponential model or use a finer time increment to find a solution.

Suggestions or Further Study

I hope some of the math presented herein can be transferred to the classroom for practical exercises. Some of my ideas for possible use follow. First, the equations are amenable to computer simulation. Programming the appropriate equations in a simple language like Visual Basic or Visual C# would be a good classroom exercise. Our company offers several programming tutorials (Visual Basic, Small Basic, C#, J#, and Java) that provide the skills to build such a program – see our website for details. If you do this, it is suggested that you solve the equations with a relatively small-time step (Δt) to insure physical correctness. Such simulations are very useful for 'what if?' type studies.

You could solve several problems similar to those posed earlier. Determine times to reach certain temperatures or temperature increases and decreases over various time periods. Model the thermostat operation and plot furnace activity over one day as the outside temperature varies.

Figure 3 shows one such activity plot with a thermostat e value of 2 degrees.

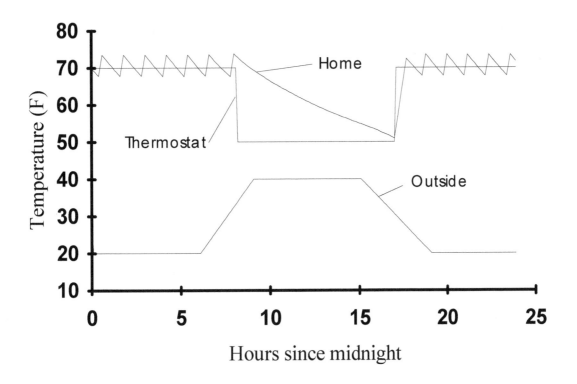

Figure 3. Typical day temperature cycles

In this case, I assumed the thermostat was at 50°F from 8 a.m. to 5 p.m. (when people aren't home) and at 70°F the rest of the time. And, I assumed the outside temperature changed linearly as shown (coldest at night, warmest during the day). Using a time step of 0.1 hours, I then computed the furnace activity and home temperature over a 24-hour period. Figure 3 plots three temperatures: thermostat setting, actual home temperature, and outside temperature. Note the variations as the furnace turns on and off and as the thermostat setting is changed. You can do similar studies. See how changing the thermostat e value affects home temperature. See how setting the thermostat back when the house is unoccupied can save furnace heating time, and hence money.

Use the furnace/heating model to do a cost analysis on the benefit of adding insulation to a home. This can be a major project. To do this, you would need to do some research on insulation costs, the costs of operating a furnace (compare gas, oil, and electric) and determining the efficiency of a furnace. Modify the equations to allow for windows. Ask at your home improvement center about appropriate R factors. I think you'll find that windows are a big heat loss. Can you compute the cost of leaving a door open for an hour during a winter's day? Can you determine how long it takes to recover the cost of additional insulation? Can you use your equations to justify replacing an old inefficient furnace with a more efficient one? Can you experimentally estimate an overall R factor for your home? Can you modify the equations to do the air conditioning (home cooling) problem? An air conditioner is like a furnace, only it removes heat from the house. I'm sure you can come up with lots of ways to use the home heating equations.

3. Satellite Orbit Problems

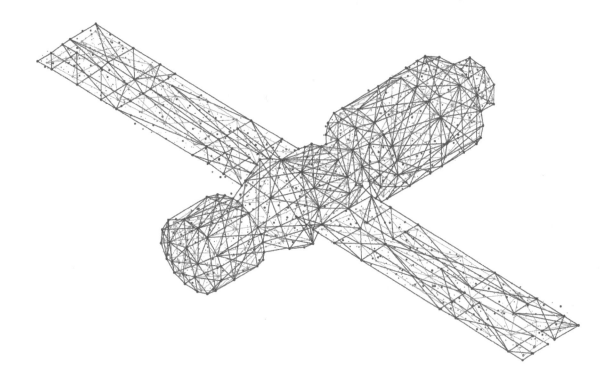

Introduction

Satellites in orbit around the earth are commonplace. They are used to transmit television signals, telephone calls, weather data, airplane navigational information, and radio programs. And, many of today's cars are equipped with GPS (global positioning satellite) locators that help them get around in traffic! Manned satellites, such as the Space Shuttle, allow for all types of valuable experimentation and space repair work. In this article, we look at some of the mathematics and physics behind satellite orbits.

We first answer the question of why satellites orbit by discussing the dynamics of satellites. Then, we examine typical orbit problems, such as how to establish an orbit and how to move from one orbit to another. Many example problems and suggestions for further work are provided.

Why Satellites Orbit

We can best explain satellite orbits by using an example. Assume we have an object (ball or rock) attached to the end of a rubber band. As you hold one end of the rubber band and swing the object around in a circle, the object tends to move away and stretch the rubber band. As the rubber band stretches, it tends to pull the object back toward your hand. The rubber band stretches in and out depending on how fast you swing the object. If you swing it fast, the object moves in a large circle. Slower speeds result in smaller circles. If you swing the object at a constant speed, the object moves in a circle of fixed radius, the rubber band staying stretched out at a fixed length. In this constant speed condition, the pull of the rubber band is equal to the pull of the object away from your hand - the object has zero net pull, hence no net acceleration. The object is in orbit.

A satellite in orbit has no net acceleration. That's why astronauts appear weightless. As a satellite spins around the earth, it tends to move away from the earth, but the force of gravity tends to bring it back to earth (kind of an invisible rubber band). When the tendency to pull away is balanced by gravity, the satellite remains in a fixed radius orbit around the earth. Figure 1 will help us develop the mathematics of satellite orbits.

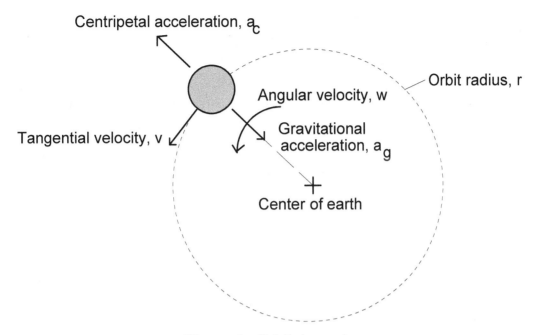

Figure 1. Orbit dynamics

A satellite is r (miles) from the center of the earth and moving around the earth at an angular velocity w (radians/hour). Tangential velocity v (miles/hour) is defined by

$$v = rw$$

There are two accelerations acting on the satellite. The spinning satellite tends to move away from the earth due to centripetal acceleration (a_c - miles/hour^2) which is defined in terms of v by

$$a_c = v^2/r$$

and in terms of w by

$$a_c = rw^2$$

Note the faster a satellite orbits, the greater the centripetal acceleration. Gravitational acceleration (a_g - miles/hour^2) tends to pull the satellite back toward the earth, and depends on how far the satellite is from earth:

25

$$a_g = \mu/r^2$$

where μ is a gravitational constant. Before looking further at μ, note that the earth acts as a "negative rubber band." With a normal rubber band, the farther you stretch it, the more it pulls back. Note that gravitational acceleration (and hence its pull) gets smaller as r gets larger!

The gravitational constant μ (miles^3/hour^2) is defined by

$$\mu = G(m_s + m_e)$$

where G is a universal constant, m_s is the satellite mass, and m_e is the mass of the earth. I think we'd all agree that the earth's mass is much greater than any satellite's mass, so for our work we can assume zero satellite mass. With this, we will define μ as

$$\mu = Gm_e$$

Now, let's look at computing the dynamics of a satellite in orbit.

Recall orbit is attained when there is no net acceleration on the satellite. In this case, the centripetal acceleration is balanced by the gravitational acceleration. Using the defined expressions, in terms of v and r, this occurs when

$$a_c = v^2/r = \mu/r^2 = a_g$$

This expression tells us that there is a unique one-to-one relationship between r (orbit radius) and v (tangential velocity) for a satellite orbit. Hence, knowing r, we can compute v

$$v = (\mu/r)^{1/2}$$

Conversely, knowing v, can compute r:

$$r = \mu/v^2$$

Note the velocity decreases as r increases. That is, the farther a satellite is from earth, the slower it moves (a result of the "negative rubber band" effect of the earth's gravitational pull).

Similar orbital expressions can be found using the angular speed w. In a balanced condition,

$$a_c = rw^2 = \mu/r^2 = a_g$$

Solving this for w yields

$$w = (\mu/r^3)^{1/2}$$

and for r, we obtain

$$r = (\mu/w^2)^{1/3}$$

Now, let's use these equations to solve some typical satellite orbit problems.

Typical Problems

In this section, we pose and solve several typical orbit problems. These can be adapted for classroom use.

Gravitational Acceleration

What is the acceleration of gravity on the surface of the earth? Our equations tell us that a_g is given by:

$$a_g = \mu/r^2$$

To evaluate this, we need values for μ and r. Recall μ is further defined by:

$$\mu = Gm_e$$

The universal gravitational constant is (found from handbooks)

$$G = 3.0227 \times 10^{-12} \text{ miles}^3/\text{hour}^2\text{-slug}$$

and the mass of the earth is (a good discussion topic is how would you ever find out such a value)

$$m_e = 4.089 \times 10^{23} \text{ slugs}$$

Yes, the proper unit of mass here is called a slug! Hence, μ is (we'll use this value for all our problems)

$$\mu = 1.2360 \times 10^{12} \text{ miles}^3/\text{hour}^2$$

Now, we need r. Recall r is measured from the center of the earth, so to find the acceleration on the surface of the earth, r is simply the earth's radius

$$r = r_e = 3960 \text{ miles}$$

Surface gravitational acceleration is thus:

$$a_g = \mu/r^2 = (1.2360 \times 10^{12} \text{ miles}^3/\text{hour}^2)/(3960 \text{ miles})^2$$

or,

$$a_g = 78{,}818 \text{ miles/hour}^2 = 32.1 \text{ feet/second}^2$$

This means if you drop something off a building, within three seconds, it is traveling 96.3 feet/second or nearly 65 miles per hour! That's why we shouldn't drop things off a building!

Orbital Velocities

How fast is the Space Shuttle traveling when it is in a 150 mile orbit above the earth? Orbital velocity is given by

$$v = (\mu/r)^{1/2}$$

Or, substituting values (again, recall r is distance from the center of the earth, hence we add r_e to the satellite altitude to get r)

$$v = [(1.2360 \times 10^{12} \text{ miles}^3/\text{hour}^2)/(3960 + 150 \text{ miles})]^{1/2} = 17{,}342 \text{ miles/hour}$$

They're really zipping along up there!

How fast is the moon moving in its orbit around the earth? The moon is about 240,000 miles above the earth, so:

$$v = (\mu/r)^{1/2} = [1.2360 \times 10^{12}/(3960 + 240000)]^{1/2} = 2,251 \text{ miles/hour}$$

One word about this result. Recall in evaluating μ, we ignored the mass of the satellite because satellites are usually small compared to the earth. Is it okay to ignore the mass of the moon here? It depends on how accurate you want to be. The earth's mass is about 81 times the mass of the moon, so the answer here is accurate to within 1 or 2 percent. If you need more accuracy, you would need to recompute a value for μ using both moon and earth mass.

Orbital Periods

How long does it take the Space Shuttle to circle the earth in a 150 mile orbit? This time, the orbital period T, is related to the angular velocity w, which is in units of radians/hour. A complete orbit encompasses 2π radians. T is the time required to complete an orbit at a rate w:

$$T = 2\pi/w$$

and since $v = rw$, an alternate expression is

$$T = 2\pi r/v$$

For a 150 mile orbit, we found earlier that $v = 17,342$ miles/hour, hence the period is

$$T = 2\pi(3960 + 150 \text{ miles})/(17342 \text{ miles/hour}) = 1.489 \text{ hours} = 89.3 \text{ minutes}$$

It takes just about an hour and a half to circle the globe. Like we said, the astronauts are really zipping along!

How long does it take the moon to circle the earth? Remember we found the moon's tangential velocity is v = 2,251 miles/hour and it is 240,000 miles above the earth, so

$$T = 2\pi(3960 + 240000)/(2251) = 681 \text{ hours} = 28.4 \text{ days}$$

This seems correct since we know there is a full moon every 28 days or so. Recall this value is slightly in error since we neglected the moon mass in computing gravitational acceleration.

Required Orbit

At what orbital altitude does the satellite period match the period of the earth's rotation? In such an orbit, the satellite "follows" the earth as it rotates, hence it remains fixed over one position on earth. We call such an orbit a geosynchronous orbit. We put communications satellites in geosynchronous orbits.

We want to know what r corresponds to a period of T = 24 hours, the amount of time for the earth to complete a rotation around its axis. First, the corresponding angular velocity is

$$w = 2\pi/T = 2\pi/(24 \text{ hours}) = 0.2618 \text{ radians/hour}$$

And, earlier, we found that the orbital radius r is related to w by

$$r = (\mu/w^2)^{1/3}$$

So,

$$r = [(1.2360 \times 10^{12} \text{ miles}^3/\text{hour}^2/(0.2618 \text{ radians/hour})^2]^{1/3} = 26{,}224 \text{ miles}$$

And, accounting for the earth's radius, we find the altitude is

$$r_{geo} = r - 3960 = 22,264 \text{ miles}$$

So, a satellite in geosynchronous orbit is over 22,000 miles above the surface of the earth! That's how far satellite television signals must travel. The corresponding angular velocity (see if you can find this) is $v = 6,865$ miles/hour.

Orbit Transfers

Now, we'll look at a very interesting mathematics problem related to orbital flight. Many times, a satellite is in one orbit and we want to move it to another orbit. Why do we want to do this? Perhaps the Space Shuttle, in one orbit, needs to rescue a satellite in another orbit. Or, we want to dock with the Space Station which is in a different orbit. Prior to moving it to a geosynchronous orbit, communication satellites are usually put in a lower orbit (a parking orbit of around 100 to 200 miles) around the earth. They are then moved to the outer orbit ($r_{geo} = 22,264$ miles).

How do we do an orbit transfer? Recall the radius (r) of an orbit is specified completely by the satellite tangential speed (v). Thus, if we change the speed, the radius will change just like our ball on a rubber band. With earth's gravity, we have seen that slower speeds result in larger radius orbits and faster speeds move the satellite closer to earth. Satellites can be equipped with small rocket engines that adjust tangential speed by applying an acceleration in the desired direction, either forward to speed up or reverse to slow down. Actually, the rocket engines produce a thrust which is directly related to acceleration by Newton's law. Let's look at a couple of examples.

Example 1 - Simple Orbit Transfer

A satellite is in an orbit with radius r_1. We want to transfer it to an orbit with radius r_2. The satellite can change its tangential velocity by applying a constant tangential acceleration A (due to thrust generated by rocket engines). How long do we apply the acceleration to move from one orbit to the other? We want to compute the engine burn time, T_{burn}.

At r_1, the satellite velocity is

$$v_1 = (\mu/r_1)^{1/2}$$

and at the new orbit (r_2), the velocity must be

$$v_2 = (\mu/r_2)^{1/2}$$

With a constant acceleration A, the time required to go from v_1 to v_2 is simply

$$T_{burn} = (v_2 - v_1)/A$$

Note if $v_2 < v_1$ (corresponding to $r_2 > r_1$ where we move from a smaller radius orbit to a larger radius orbit), A must be a negative number to yield a positive burn time. Otherwise, A is positive.

Say we want to move a satellite from a 500 mile (altitude) orbit to a 1000 mile orbit and our rockets generate a tangential acceleration of -150 miles/hour^2. How long will it take? First, the corresponding tangential velocities are

$$v_1 = [(1.2360 \times 10^{12}/(3960 + 500)]^{1/2} = 16{,}647 \text{ miles/hour}$$
$$v_2 = [(1.2360 \times 10^{12}/(3960 + 1000)]^{1/2} = 15{,}786 \text{ miles/hour}$$

So, the burn time is

$$T_{burn} = (v_2 - v_1)/A = (15786 - 16647)/(-150) = 5.740 \text{ hours}$$

It takes 5.740 hours to complete the orbit transfer. Let's plot the trajectory followed by the satellite as it moves from one orbit to the other.

Figure 2 shows the orbital plane with the coordinates we will use to locate a satellite in space.

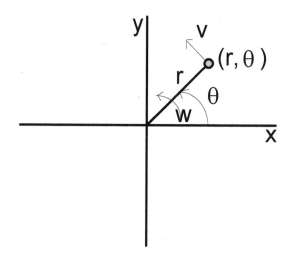

Figure 2. Satellite coordinates

The satellite traveling at tangential velocity v (angular velocity w) has a location (r, θ) where r is the orbit radius and θ the position angle as measured from the arbitrary x axis. Let's find the time variation of r and θ for a satellite undergoing a constant acceleration. If the satellite undergoes a tangential acceleration A, the time variation of the velocity is

$$v(t) = v_o + At$$

where t is time and v_o is the satellite velocity when the acceleration begins (v at t = 0). As v changes, a new orbit is established with the corresponding radius

34

$$r(t) = \mu/v^2(t) = \mu/(v_o + At)^2$$

With these, the angular velocity at t is

$$w(t) = v(t)/r(t)$$

We still need to find $\theta(t)$, which presents a problem. Since $w(t)$ (the rate at which θ changes) is not constant, integral calculus is required to develop an exact expression for $\theta(t)$. We'll avoid such mathematics by making an approximation. To evaluate $\theta(t)$, we will use the average value of w from t = 0 to the current time t. This yields

$$\theta(t) = \theta_o + \tfrac{1}{2}[w(t) + w_o]t$$

where θ_o and w_o are the values of θ and w, respectively, when the acceleration begins (t = 0).

We now use these equations to plot the trajectory followed by the satellite in our example orbit transfer. For this example, A = -150 miles/hour^2 and t will range from 0 to T_{burn}. Initial values (prior to applying the acceleration) are:

$$v_o = v_1 = 16{,}647 \text{ miles/hour}$$
$$w_o = w_1 = v_1/r_1 = 3.7325 \text{ radians/hour}$$

Figure 3 plots the resulting trajectory (we assume $\theta_o = 0$). Note the satellite follows a spiral like trajectory, orbiting the earth three times, until it enters the 1000 mile orbit. At t = T_{burn}, we find $v(T_{burn})$ = v_2 and $r(T_{burn})$ = r_2, as we would expect. When the satellite enters the larger orbit, $\theta(T_{burn})$ = 19.847 radians. Subtracting 6π (3 orbits) from this value yields $\theta(T_{burn})$ = 0.997 radians = 57.1 degrees. This point is indicated on Figure 3.

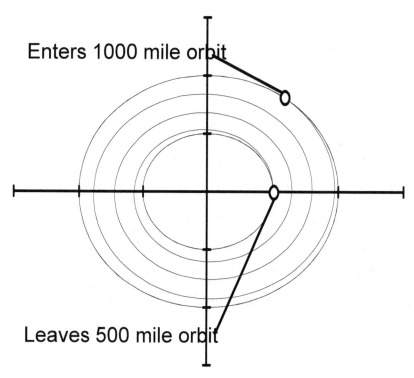

Figure 3. Simple orbit transfer (satellite altitude)

Example 2- Satellite Rendezvous

This problem is like the previous example except that, in addition to changing the orbital radius, we also want to fix the angular position where we enter the new orbit. This is the rendezvous problem. Rendezvous is used by the Space Shuttle to rescue damaged satellites and will be used by future astronauts to dock with the Space Station.

Figure 4 illustrates the problem as we begin the rendezvous process. A satellite is in orbit with radius r_1, velocity v_1, angular velocity w_1, and initial angular position θ_{10}. We want to move this satellite to an orbit of radius r_2. That orbit has a corresponding tangential velocity v_2 and angular velocity w_2. The desired rendezvous point is defined by the initial angle θ_{20}.

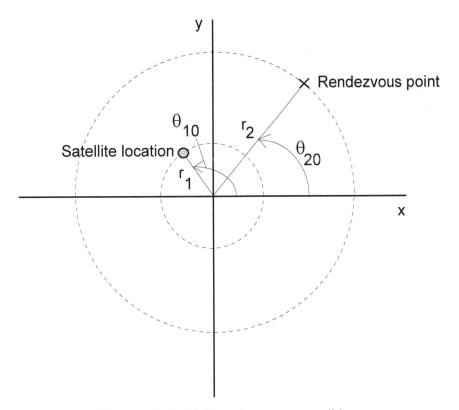

Figure 4. Initial rendezvous conditions

(The sketch in Figure 4 assumes $r_2 > r_1$ - the mathematics developed here also apply if $r_1 < r_2$). In the previous example, we found the accelerating (or decelerating) burn time to move from one orbit to another. That time still applies here. It will still take T_{burn} units of time to move from r_1 to r_2. Knowing T_{burn}, we also computed how much the angular position changes as we move from one orbit to another. That angular change will be the same. In the rendezvous problem, beginning with the known configuration in Figure 4, we wait T_{wait} units of time (we need to find this value) until the satellite and the rendezvous point (which rotate at rates w_1 and w_2, respectively) are separated by the relative angular distance we know the satellite will traverse during the burn. Then, after this wait, we burn the satellite rocket engines T_{burn} units of time. That insures that, at the end of the burn, the satellite and rendezvous point are coincident.

Mathematically, we require the angular position of the satellite and the angular position of the rendezvous point to match at the end of the two phase (wait, then burn) rendezvous. Let's develop those equations and find what T_{wait} yields a rendezvous. The rendezvous point moves at a constant angular velocity w_2 (related directly to r_2) during both the wait and burn phase, hence the final rendezvous point position, θ_r, is

$$\theta_r = \theta_{20} + w_2(T_{wait} + T_{burn})$$

The satellite rotates at rate w_1 during the wait phase, then (again, avoiding integral calculus) at the average of w_1 and w_2 during the burn phase. So, satellite position at the end of the rendezvous, θ_s, is

$$\theta_s = \theta_{10} + w_1 T_{wait} + \tfrac{1}{2}(w_1 + w_2)T_{burn}$$

Equating θ_s with θ_r and solving for T_{wait} yields

$$T_{wait} = (\theta_{10} - \theta_{20})/(w_2 - w_1) - \tfrac{1}{2}T_{burn}$$

This time specifies how long to wait in orbit r_1 before firing the rockets that change the satellite velocity and move it to orbit r_2.

Before trying an example, we need to look at the T_{wait} expression a little closer. T_{wait} must be positive (how can you wait a negative amount of time?) but notice there is no guarantee this will be true. For example, if $\theta_{10} = \theta_{20}$, T_{wait} will be $-\tfrac{1}{2}T_{burn}$. What do we do? The solution to this problem lies in the fact that the angular difference can be offset by any integer multiple of 2π. That is, a difference of π radians is the same as a difference of 3π or $-\pi$ radians. So, if T_{wait} turns out to be negative, we can keep adding $\pm 2\pi/(w_2 - w_1)$ to T_{wait} until it becomes positive and still be able to achieve rendezvous. We choose the positive sign in this additive term if $w_2 > w_1$, the negative sign if $w_2 < w_1$. Now, let's look at an example.

We will use the same conditions as before. That is, the satellite is in a 500 mile (altitude) radius orbit and we want to move to a 1000 mile orbit. Hence,

$$r_1 = 3960 + 500 = 4460 \text{ miles}$$
$$r_2 = 3960 + 1000 = 4960 \text{ miles}$$

Corresponding velocities at these orbits are:

$$v_1 = 16{,}647 \text{ miles/hour}$$
$$w_1 = v_1/r_1 = 3.7326 \text{ radians/hour}$$
$$v_2 = 15{,}786 \text{ miles/hour}$$
$$w_2 = v_2/r_2 = 3.1826 \text{ radians/hour}$$

Lastly, we assume that at the beginning of rendezvous,

$$\theta_{10} = \theta_{20} = 0$$

In the previous example, for an acceleration of $A = -150$ miles/hour^2, we found T_{burn} = 5.740 hours. Now, let's find T_{wait}.

The wait time is given by

$$T_{wait} = (\theta_{10} - \theta_{20})/(w_2 - w_1) - \tfrac{1}{2}T_{burn}$$

or substituting values, we find:

$$T_{wait} = (0 - 0)/(3.1826 - 3.7326) - \tfrac{1}{2}(5.740) = -2.870 \text{ hours}$$

Since T_{wait} is negative, we add $-2\pi/(3.1826 - 3.7326) = 11.424$ hours to the computed value, or

$$T_{wait} = 8.554 \text{ hours}$$

So, to achieve rendezvous, the satellite remains in it's r_1 orbit for 8.554 hours before entering the burn phase.

Let's check our answer by computing the final satellite and rendezvous point angular locations (we know the orbital radii will match). The final rendezvous location is

$$\theta_r = \theta_{20} + w_2(T_{wait} + T_{burn}) = 0 + 3.1826(8.554 + 5.740) = 45.492 \text{ radians}$$

or equivalently (compensating for the number of rotations made during rendezvous, i.e. subtracting 2π multiples)

$$\theta_r = 1.510 \text{ radians} = 86.5 \text{ degrees}$$

Final satellite location is

$$\theta_s = \theta_{10} + w_1 T_{wait} + \tfrac{1}{2}(w_1 + w_2)T_{burn}$$
$$= 0 + 3.7326(8.554) + \tfrac{1}{2}(3.7326 + 3.1826)(5.740) = 51.775 \text{ radians}$$

or compensating for orbits completed,

$$\theta_s = 1.510 \text{ radians} = 86.5 \text{ degrees}$$

The two angles are the same - a successful rendezvous!! The rendezvous path is plotted in Figure 5.

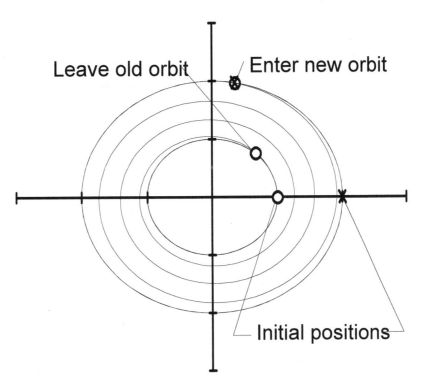

Figure 5. Satellite rendezvous

Concluding Remarks

The equations relating tangential and angular speed and orbital radius for a satellite orbiting the earth have been developed and some sample problems have been presented. Such equations provide a good basis for several classroom studies. Before looking at potential areas for further work, a word of caution. The equations presented here are a simplification of actual orbital mathematics. We have considered only centripetal acceleration when there are other accelerating forces in action. We have used a very simple gravity model. We assume that the satellite instantaneously moves to a new orbit as the velocity changes. We have assumed circular orbits - they are usually elliptical. I point out these assumptions to make you aware there is more to the problem than what is covered here. Even with these simplifications, however, the mathematics yield many interesting problems. Some of my ideas follow.

41

With the simple gravity model, plot the variation of gravitational acceleration with altitude above earth. Does it change very quickly? Can you develop an even simpler model? Plot tangential and angular velocity versus orbital radius. Describe any trends. Recompute the moon's dynamics by including the moon mass in the μ term. Is there a significant difference? Plot orbital periods versus orbital radius. You should be able to come up with many problems using the equations relating v, w, and r.

The orbit transfer problem, and particularly the rendezvous problem, offers many avenues for further study. Input the initial satellite and rendezvous point conditions. Compute T_{wait} and T_{burn}. Compute the final orbital radii and angular positions. They should match. Can you program the computer to plot the satellite and rendezvous point positions during the rendezvous process? Can you think of other ways of plotting the computed results to demonstrate the rendezvous? Can you think of other ways to do a rendezvous? In the example we looked at, we assumed a constant known acceleration. Can you resolve the problem by finding the acceleration that will yield a desired rendezvous?

Another interesting topic involves the accuracy of our solution. In our example, we assumed perfect measurements of initial positions and assumed we knew our acceleration exactly. Actually, there are errors in these values due to instrument inaccuracies and due to manufacturing defects in making the accelerating rockets. This means our rendezvous solution will also be inaccurate. We will not achieve rendezvous. Can you develop a rendezvous procedure that accounts for these inaccuracies? A possible approach is to try the solution you develop and see how close you come to rendezvous. Based on how far you are from the rendezvous point, you may need to make some fine orbit adjustments (small accelerations and decelerations) to make corrections to satellite position. This is what is done in actual rendezvous. As the satellite (or Shuttle) gets closer and closer to the desired point, small course corrections are made to account for any errors noted.

A last topic for study requires some knowledge of calculus. Recall in our orbit transfer examples, we had to develop approximate relations for the variation in satellite angular position as it moved from one orbit to another. We assumed an average angular velocity. See if you can develop an exact relation - it involves integrating the time variation of w during the rocket engine burn process. For the rendezvous problem, the exact expression for the satellite angular position is (at least the form I found):

$$\theta_s = \theta_{10} + w_1 T_{wait} + (v_2^4 - v_1^4)/4\mu A$$

Check how the approximate and exact values compare. Will using the approximate value result in major errors? I claim it will. For the rendezvous example, if you use the wait time computed using the approximate expression and perform the rendezvous, there will be an error of 0.019 radians between satellite and rendezvous point locations. This doesn't seem like a lot. But, at a radius of 4960 miles (1000 mile orbit plus the earth's radius), this translates into an error of over 94 miles! It would be difficult to rescue a satellite with such an error. If we used the approximate expression, we would need to use some kind of mid-course correction procedure as described above. In real problems, we strive for the utmost in accuracy in all calculations, measurements, and maneuvers to insure precise dockings and rendezvous.

4. Pendulums and Complex Numbers

Introduction

In the study of quadratic equations, we are introduced to the concepts of imaginary and complex numbers. A common question is: why do we have to worry about imaginary numbers? After all, if they're imaginary, they don't exist! This chapter gives a real-world example of the use of complex numbers and shows how they relate to real quantities.

We will show how a quadratic equation (and complex numbers) can be used to model the dynamics of a swinging pendulum. Equations for both a normal and an upside-down (inverted) pendulum are developed. We also discuss how we can use mathematics to balance an inverted pendulum (the same concept used in every rocket and missile launch in history). Hopefully, the equations presented can provide a springboard for classroom simulation studies.

Pendulum Motion

In this section, we will develop the equations that describe the motion of a swinging pendulum. The equations may be simple, but they actually have a wide variety of real applications from oscillators to rocket launches. The pendulum we'll work with is shown in Figure 1.

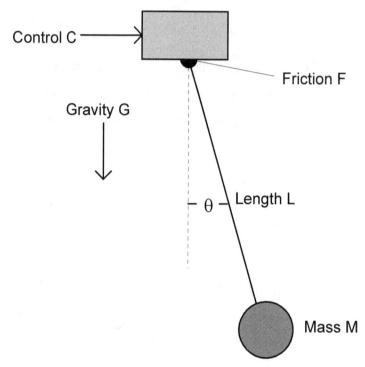

Figure 1. Pendulum system

It consists of a mass (M) attached to a stick of length L. The angular distance from vertical is designated θ. We assume the stick is massless. It is assumed that there is some friction in the pivot with coefficient F. Gravity (G) acts on the pendulum mass. For completeness, we assume a control acceleration (C) is being applied to the pendulum pivot mount. All such dynamic systems have an equation which describes how that system changes with time - a so-called "characteristic equation." With all of the above assumptions, the pendulum system's characteristic equation is (obtained by applying Newton's law to the pendulum):

$$(Ls^2 + Fs + G)\theta = -C\theta$$

The C term is negative because it acts to decrease the angular displacement θ - this will become clearer later. Note this equation is second-order in the solution variables.

Based on what values the roots of this equation take on, we have different descriptions of the pendulum motion. For now, we will neglect the control C (i.e., C = 0). With that, the quadratic equation tells us that the two roots of the characteristic equation are

$$s_1 = \{-F + (F^2 - 4LG)^{1/2}\}/2L$$
$$s_2 = \{-F - (F^2 - 4LG)^{1/2}\}/2L$$

Looking at these roots, we notice two possibilities. The term in the square root could be positive giving us two real roots, or it could be negative giving us complex roots. Actually, there is also a third possibility where the square root term could be zero, but we won't worry about that case here. Each possibility yields different pendulum motion.

Pendulum Motion - Real Roots

Note the first possibility, a positive term in the square root, occurs when

$$F^2 > 4LG$$

or when we have a lot of friction. This is called an overdamped response and, if we pull the pendulum back an amount θ_o from vertical, the pendulum displacement as a function of time (t) is given by (to find this equation requires calculus skills – don't worry how we got it)

$$\theta(t) = \theta_0[s_2\exp(s_1t) - s_1\exp(s_2t)]/(s_2-s_1)$$

where the exponential operator (exp) is defined by

$$\exp(a) = e^a$$

where ($e \approx 2.718281828$). The corresponding angular speed (the time rate of change of displacement) is

$$\omega(t) = \theta_0 s_1 s_2[\exp(s_1t) - \exp(s_2t)]/(s_2-s_1)$$

What does this response look like? First, notice if either s_1 or s_2 is a positive number, $\theta(t)$ will grow exponentially as t increases. Physical intuition tells us this is impossible and if we look closely, we see neither root can be positive (as long as we have positive friction, or F > 0). As an example, let's use θ_0 = 20 degrees, G = 32.2 feet per second per second, and L = 1.5 feet. With these numbers, we have overdamped response whenever F > 13.9.

Figures 2(a) and 2(b) show pendulum response (displacement and speed) for F = 50, a lot of friction.

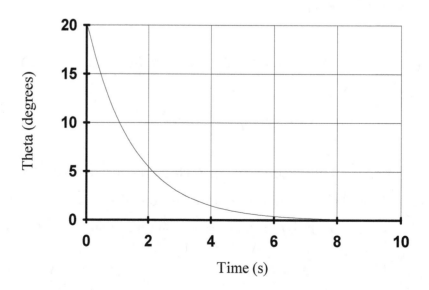

Figure 2(a). Pendulum overdamped displacement

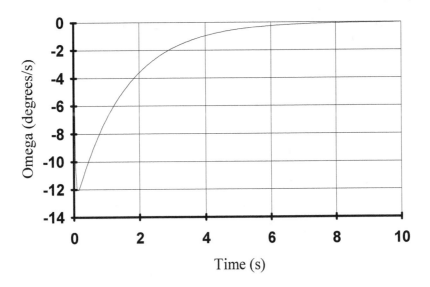

Time (s)

Figure 2(b). Pendulum overdamped speed

Note the curve looks like you would expect. With a lot of friction, the pendulum just goes slowly to the θ(t) = 0 point, never oscillating at all. This case is called overdamped because it has so much damping (friction) that it does not oscillate like a pendulum should. What happens if we don't have a lot of friction? This is called the underdamped case and here's where the complex numbers come into play.

Pendulum Motion - Complex Roots

The second possibility for the roots of the characteristic equation occurs when

$$F^2 < 4LG$$

that is, we have less friction, allowing the pendulum to oscillate. In this underdamped case, we have complex roots

$$s_1 = \{-F + i(4LG - F^2)^{1/2}\}/2L$$
$$s_2 = \{-F - i(4LG - F^2)^{1/2}\}/2L$$

where recall i is the square root of negative one (-1). For simplicity, we will define a damping factor D

$$D = -F/2L$$

and an oscillation frequency W

$$W = (4LG - F^2)^{1/2}/2L$$

such that

$$s_1 = D + iW$$
$$s_2 = D - iW$$

With these definitions, the pendulum displacement and angular speed are now described by (again, these come from calculus)

$$\theta(t) = \theta_o \exp(Dt)[\cos(Wt) - (D/W)\sin(Wt)]$$
$$\omega(t) = -\theta_o \exp(Dt)[W + (D^2/W)]\sin(Wt)$$

Notice with the sine and cosine terms, there will be oscillations. Note in particular that the real part of the complex roots (D) tells us about the damping, or friction, that is present while the imaginary part (W) tells us how fast the pendulum will oscillate. The real and imaginary parts have physical meaning.

An actual pendulum will have a slightly lower W than that computed here. Recall we neglected the stick mass - by doing this we assume that the mass on the end of the stick is much larger than stick mass. This also completely eliminates mass from the characteristic equation (note no M term). We can still use our equations however, with a slight adjustment. What we usually do is measure the frequency of the actual pendulum and compute an "effective length" such that the frequency matches the theoretical value. This "effective length" is usually close to the actual value. Note too that D is negative, insuring a decaying response. Different values of D will yield different response shapes - all of them will be decaying sinusoids.

Figures 3(a) and 3(b) how the pendulum responds with F = 1. This isn't a really spectacular result.

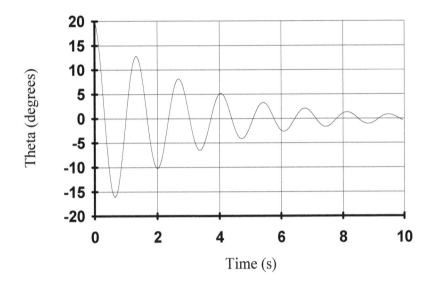

Figure 3(a). Pendulum underdamped displacement

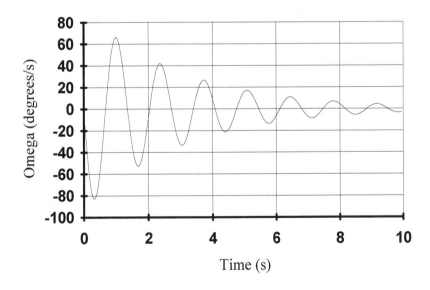

Figure 3(b). Pendulum underdamped speed

A pretty spiral (Figure 4) results if you plot angular speed versus displacement.

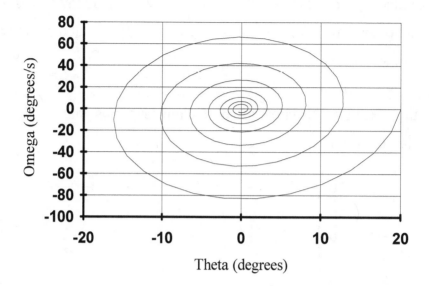

Figure 4. Pendulum underdamped phase plane plot

Such a plot is called a phase plane plot. Using these two equations, different phase plane plots can be obtained by playing with the friction coefficient F. For example, what would the phase plane plot look like if F = 0?

Though they make pretty plots, the pendulum equations given are really uninteresting. The pendulum merely oscillates back and forth eventually decaying to zero. We can make it an interesting problem though by simply turning the pendulum upside down (an inverted pendulum).

Inverted Pendulum Motion

The new problem is sketched in Figure 5. We want to balance the pendulum using the control C. Don't think this is a silly problem - the mathematics and concepts presented here are basically the same as those used in every rocket and missile control system to insure proper flight path alignments.

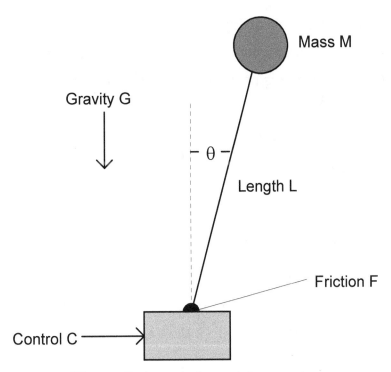

Figure 5. Inverted pendulum system

This configuration reverses the sign on the gravity term in the characteristic equation. This makes sense - in the normal pendulum, gravity acts to bring the pendulum to zero displacement where now gravity will try to make the pendulum fall. So, the new characteristic equation is

$$(Ls^2 + Fs - G)\theta = -C\theta$$

Notice if C = 0, the roots of this equation are

$$s_1 = \{-F + (F^2 + 4LG)^{1/2}\}/2L$$
$$s_2 = \{-F - (F^2 + 4LG)^{1/2}\}/2L$$

and, since these are real and not complex roots, the displacement response is

$$\theta(t) = \theta_o[s_2exp(s_1t) - s_1exp(s_2t)]/(s_2-s_1)$$

This looks like our previously defined overdamped response with one big difference that is not obvious. Before, both s_1 and s_2 were negative numbers giving a decaying exponential. Now notice s_1 is positive (s_2 is still negative) and $\theta(t)$ grows with time; that is, the pendulum falls over! That's what we would expect, isn't it? So, to keep the pendulum from falling over, we need some control. C cannot be zero.

With a non zero C, we rewrite the characteristic equation as

$$[Ls^2 + Fs + (C - G)]\theta = 0$$

This is essentially the same equation we used in the noninverted case (G is replaced by C - G), so all of the analysis we did before still holds (just watch signs!). The roots of this equation are

$$s_1 = \{-F + [F^2 - 4L(C - G)]^{1/2}\}/2L$$
$$s_2 = \{-F - [F^2 - 4L(C - G)]^{1/2}\}/2L$$

Inverted Pendulum Motion - Real Roots

We will get an overdamped response (real roots) when

$$F^2 > 4L(C - G)$$

and the pendulum displacement is given by

$$\theta(t) = \theta_0[s_2\exp(s_1t) - s_1\exp(s_2t)]/(s_2-s_1)$$

We just saw the pendulum will fall over if s_1 is positive. Looking at the above roots, note s_1 will be negative if

$$C > G$$

That is, the control value C must be greater than G. If we don't apply enough control, the pendulum will still fall over! If C is indeed greater than G, the pendulum is balanced with an overdamped response.

Inverted Pendulum Motion - Complex Roots

We will get complex roots (underdamped response) when

$$F^2 < 4L(C - G)$$

or when the control meets the criteria

$$C > F^2/4L + G$$

So, with larger amounts of control C, we can induce oscillations. This underdamped response is the same as for the noninverted pendulum

$$\theta(t) = \theta_o \exp(Dt)[\cos(Wt) - (D/W)\sin(Wt)]$$
$$\omega(t) = -\theta_o \exp(Dt)[W + (D^2/W)]\sin(Wt)$$

with the same damping factor

$$D = -F/2L$$

but a new oscillation frequency W

$$W = [4L(C - G) - F^2]^{1/2}/2L$$

So, we can control the inverted pendulum and make it balance. A value for C is selected by the designer to provide a desired response. We see that C must be at least greater than G to balance the pendulum. For higher C values, response remains overdamped until C exceeds $F^2/2L + G$, when it becomes underdamped.

One last point to address involves the physical interpretation of C, the control coefficient. Intuitively, what we try to do is apply an acceleration to the pendulum base, pushing it in the direction the pendulum is falling. That is, we try to "catch" the pendulum. Mathematically, we apply an acceleration proportional to how far the pendulum is from vertical. If the pendulum is nearly balanced, we apply a small acceleration. If it is far from vertical, we apply a large acceleration. The proportionality constant used in this "control law" is the value C. Hence, the bigger C is, the larger the possible accelerations.

Concluding Remarks

Equations describing the motion of both noninverted and inverted pendulums were developed. We saw that, depending on the type of characteristic equation roots (real or complex), different pendulum motions were possible. We also developed methods for balancing an inverted pendulum. These equations can be used for several classroom exercises.

Discuss the general problem of using mathematics to describe the motion of physical systems. Discuss how to check that the mathematics are true representations of the motion. For the pendulum, we could always use intuition to check the equations. It is intuitively satisfying to note that when there is a lot of friction, we obtained a response that corresponded to a lot of friction. Similarly, with small amounts of friction, the equations correctly predicted the expected oscillations. Can you develop similar equations for other dynamic systems?

Program the equations on a computer. Develop a simulation of both the noninverted and inverted pendulums for different root types. Study pendulum response as the various parameters (friction, length, control) are changed.

Have students describe how a pendulum works - what makes it oscillate? It's all related to potential and kinetic energy and losses associated with friction. Where are pendulums, or similar oscillating devices, used?

It might be fun to build a real pendulum and see how its performance relates to the simulated pendulum - it's probably easiest to study the noninverted pendulum. I would suggest just hanging a weight on a string (remember we assumed the weight of the stick was negligible). You could compare actual pendulum frequency with the theoretical frequency given by

$$W = (4LG - F^2)^{1/2}/2L$$

57

To do this, we need to look at units of frequency. The units of the theoretical W are radians per second. The usual unit of frequency is a Hertz (abbreviated Hz) which is a cycle per second. There are 2π radians in a cycle, so the theoretical frequency in Hz is given by

$$W = (4LG - F^2)^{1/2}/4\pi L \quad [Hz]$$

Now, to get the true pendulum frequency in Hz, I suggest the following. Using a stopwatch, determine how long it takes to complete 10 complete (back and forth) cycles. The true frequency in Hz is then 10 divided by the time to complete 10 cycles. Following your comparison of measured and theoretical frequency, can you match the two values by adjusting F and/or L (remember the idea of effective length)? I'm sure you can think of more experiments of this type. Using a real system to check on a computer simulation is called model validation. It is probably the most important part of computer simulation.

5. A Look at Real-World Problem Solving

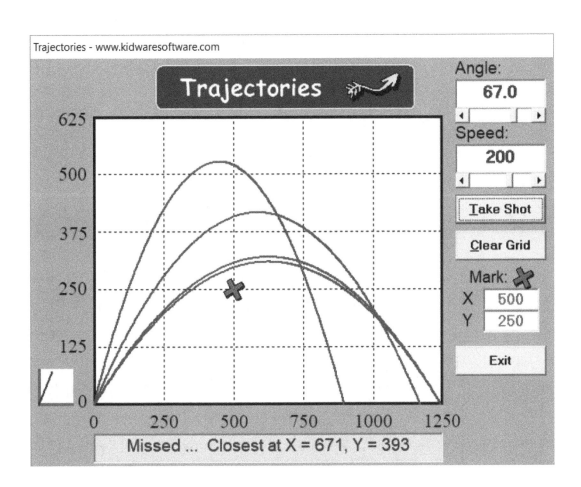

Introduction

This chapter presents an example of a real-world problem that addresses several important points in the problem-solving process.

The presented problem, illustrated in Figure 1, involves the trajectory of a projectile.

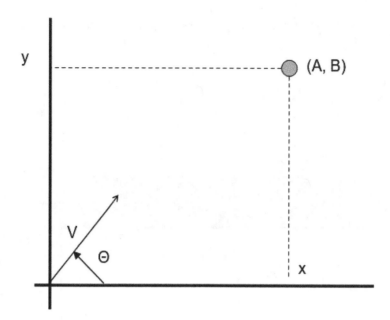

Figure 1.   Projectile trajectory problem

The projectile starts its flight at the origin of the Cartesian (xy) plane with a speed of V at an angle of Θ. The problem is to reach a desired point (A, B) by selecting V and Θ. This problem has a wide variety of real applications: rocket and missile launching, targeting and intercepts, satellite orbit transfers and rendezvous, numerical optimization, polynomial root finding, and solving nonlinear equations. The mathematics needed to solve the problem are not too involved - only algebra and trigonometry. The process of solving the problem, however, is at times detailed and tedious. But this is a concept that needs to be taught: real-world problems are not necessarily easy.

Projectile Trajectories

Referring once again to Figure 1, we have a projectile at the origin of the Cartesian (xy) plane with an initial speed of V at an angle Θ. The problem is to reach a desired point (A, B) by choosing V and Θ. We require both A and B to be positive or zero. To simplify things, assume we know V - we'll just worry about Θ (and time of flight, t).

The equations of motion for the projectile, ignoring winds, assuming only planar motion, and with gravitational acceleration (g) in the negative y direction are

$$x(t) = (Vcos\Theta)t$$
$$y(t) = (Vsin\Theta)t - \tfrac{1}{2}gt^2$$

Note x is described by the x component of speed times the time (t). And, y is the y speed component times t minus the effects of gravity. These equations are referred to as our system model. It describes our problem mathematically. Now, the question is: for known V, what Θ is needed to reach the desired point (A, B)? We need to solve the equations

$$x(t) = (Vcos\Theta)t = A$$
$$y(t) = (Vsin\Theta)t - \tfrac{1}{2}gt^2 = B$$

for two unknowns t (time of flight) and Θ (initial heading). At this point in the problem solving process, we've decided what the problem is and found all pertinent information. Let's look at whether we can solve the problem.

Before we examine ways to solve the problem, let's scope out ranges of possible solutions. This is an important step in problem solving. Obviously, it would be worthless to try to attain an impossible desired point; that is, one that is out of the projectile range. For our work here, we'll use g = 32.2 feet/second^2 and assume V = 200 feet/second. Figure 2 plots various trajectories for different values of Θ (these plots were generated using a Microsoft Excel spreadsheet). Note maximum downrange (x) is about 1250 feet and maximum altitude (y) is about 600 feet. So, we shouldn't try to go outside the area covered by these example trajectories. In solving such problems, you should always know what the range of possible solutions is. In this example, if you need to go outside a computed range, you'd have to increase the speed V, giving your projectile a little more oomph!

With the solution range scoped out, let's look at solving the problem at hand. We want to solve for the angle Θ in terms of the desired point (A, B) and the speed V. The procedure to find this expression is not elegant. We'll just write down the equations and use available trigonometric relations (from a mathematical handbook) until we obtain the desired result. Recall the two equations we have are:

$$(V\cos\Theta)t = A$$
$$(V\sin\Theta)t - \tfrac{1}{2}gt^2 = B$$

If we solve the first equation for t (time of flight) and substitute that result into the second equation, we obtain

$$A\sin\Theta/\cos\Theta - \tfrac{1}{2}g[A/(V\cos\Theta]^2 = B$$

We need to solve this equation for Θ! Multiply both sides by $\cos^2\Theta$.

$$A\sin\Theta\cos\Theta - \tfrac{1}{2}g[A/V]^2 = B\cos^2\Theta$$

Looking at our math handbook, we find the following trigonometric identities

$$\sin\Theta\cos\Theta = \tfrac{1}{2}\sin2\Theta$$
$$\cos^2\Theta = \tfrac{1}{2}(\cos2\Theta + 1)$$

Using these in the last equation results in (after collecting some terms):

$$A\sin2\Theta - B\cos2\Theta = B + g(A/V)^2$$

It seems like we should be able to solve this for 2Θ and hence Θ. And we can, by using one more trigonometric identity. This identity states:

$$\text{Asin}2\Theta - \text{Bcos}2\Theta = (A^2 + B^2)^{\frac{1}{2}}\sin[2\Theta + \tan^{-1}(-B/A)]$$

Using this identity yields:

$$B + g(A/V)^2 = (A^2 + B^2)^{\frac{1}{2}}\sin[2\Theta + \tan^{-1}(-B/A)]$$

Now, solving for Θ, we obtain the desired result:

$$\Theta = \frac{1}{2}[\sin^{-1}\{[B + g(A/V)^2]/(A^2 + B^2)^{\frac{1}{2}}\} - \tan^{-1}(-B/A)]$$

This is not a particularly pretty result, but it is correct. Before continuing, let's look a little closer at this result.

First, we need to see if a solution exists. For a value of Θ to exist, the argument within the inverse sine term must have a magnitude less than or equal to one. For our answer to make physical sense, we can only have positive values for Θ (see Figure 1). So, we can further say the argument must be positive. For that to occur, we require

$$B + g(A/V)^2 \leq (A^2 + B^2)^{\frac{1}{2}}$$

which in terms of V is

$$V^2 \geq gA^2/[(A^2 + B^2)^{\frac{1}{2}} - B]$$

This is an important expression. It tells us the minimum speed (V) required to reach a point (A, B). If V is not large enough, the projectile cannot reach the point. The case of too small a V corresponds to the area outside the potential solutions plotted

63

in Figure 2.

Having developed an existence requirement for our Θ solution, let's specify a reasonability requirement. This comes from examining the problem in Figure 1. It is obvious that Θ must be between 0 and 90 degrees - any other value would not make sense. If the expression for Θ results in an answer outside this range, we cannot use it.

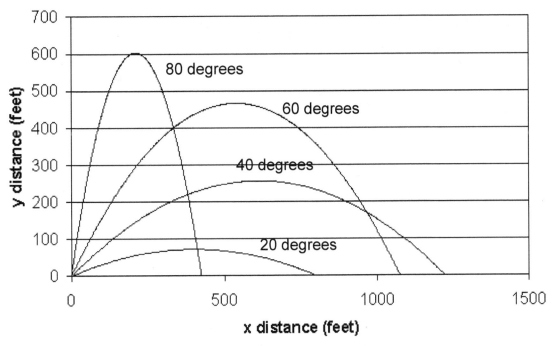

Figure 2.   Typical trajectories for various Θ

A last consideration before moving on is the possibility of multiple solutions. That is, for a given V, is there more than one value of Θ (within the range of 0 to 90 degrees) that will reach the desired point (A, B)? I claim there is and I claim there are two values of Θ that will reach a point. To back up this claim, look once again at this intermediate result in our solution process

$$B + g(A/V)^2 = (A^2 + B^2)^{1/2}\sin[2\Theta + \tan^{-1}(-B/A)]$$

Solving this for the sine term yields

$$\sin[2\Theta + \tan^{-1}(-B/A)] = B + g(A/V)^2/(A^2 + B^2)^{1/2}$$

This is the expression we used to find Θ earlier – note the right hand side of the equation does not depend on Θ. Recall for the sine function that for some angle Φ

$$\sin\Phi = \sin(180° - \Phi)$$

65

So, since the right-hand side of the expression above does not depend on Θ, if we designate our first solution as Θ_1, we see another solution for Θ (Θ_2) can be found from

$$\sin[2\Theta_1 + \tan^{-1}(-B/A)] = B + g(A/V)^2/(A^2 + B^2)^{1/2} = \sin[180° - 2\Theta_2 + \tan^{-1}(-B/A)]$$

Or, we must solve

$$\sin[2\Theta_1 + \tan^{-1}(-B/A)] = \sin[180° - 2\Theta_2 + \tan^{-1}(-B/A)]$$

for Θ_2. Or, another solution lies at

$$\boxed{\Theta_2 = 90° - \Theta_1 - \tan^{-1}(-B/A)}$$

Once both solutions are found, it is up to the analyst to decide which solution is better.

Let's look at an example. For computational purposes, we'll summarize what we've found. Assume we have a projectile with initial speed V acting under the effect of gravity g. We want to find an angle Θ that allows the projectile to reach a point (A, B). We will be able to reach that point if:

$$V^2 \geq gA^2/[(A^2 + B^2)^{1/2} - B]$$

If this requirement is met, there are two angles that reach the desired point. These angles are:

$$\Theta_1 = \tfrac{1}{2}[\sin^{-1}\{[B + g(A/V)^2]/(A^2 + B^2)^{\frac{1}{2}}\} - \tan^{-1}(-B/A)]$$

and

$$\Theta_2 = 90° - \Theta_1 - \tan^{-1}(-B/A)$$

Both Θ_1 and Θ_2 must be between 0 and 90 degrees.

Example of Projectile Trajectories

We'll still use $g = 32.2$ feet/second^2. Assume we want to reach the point (A, B) = (600, 150). To reach this point, the minimum speed required is given by

$$V^2 \geq 32.2(600)^2/[(600^2 + 150^2)^{1/2} - 150]$$

or,

$$V \geq 157.3 \text{ feet/second}$$

We'll use $V = 200$ feet/second. With this value, I compute the two solution angles as follows:

$$\Theta_1 = V^2[\sin^{-1}\{[150 + 32.2(600/200)^2]/(600^2 + 150^2)^{1/2}\} - \tan^{-1}(-150/600)]$$
$$= \tfrac{1}{2}[\sin^{-1}(0.7111) - \tan^{-1}(-0.25)]$$
$$= \tfrac{1}{2}[45.33° - (-14.04°)]$$

$$\Theta_1 = 29.68°$$

and

$$\Theta_2 = 90° - 29.68° - (-14.04°)$$

$$\Theta_2 = 74.36°$$

Both angles are positive and less than 90 degrees, so they make physical sense. We could check the answers for correctness by substituting the Θ values back into the equation relating Θ to A and B and see if it indeed is satisfied. Or, we could use the original equations for x(t) and y(t) and plot the resulting trajectories (allow time to start at zero and continue until x = A, y = B). We choose the latter option. The trajectories resulting from these two angles are plotted in Figure 3.

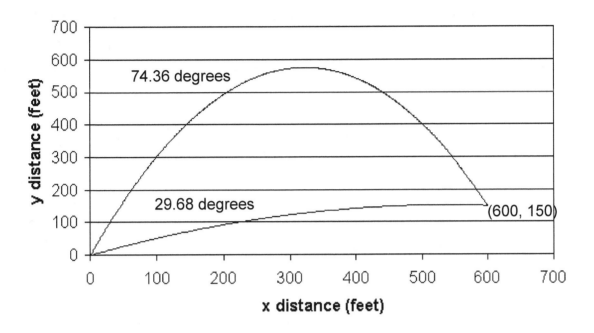

Figure 3.　　Two trajectories to (600, 150)

Examining Figure 3, we see that, as expected, both solutions achieve the desired point of (A, B) = (600, 150). The question now is which solution is better, if any? It depends on further specifications on the problem. A common criterion in projectile problems is minimum time, that is picking the trajectory that gets us there faster. This not only saves time, but fuel, which allows for bigger payloads when rockets are being guided. Applying a minimum time requirement, we would choose Θ = 29.68° (time of flight is 3.45 seconds - do you know how we found this?). But then, if there are obstacles close to the ground, we'd have to pick the "loftier" trajectory, or Θ = 74.36°

Concluding Remarks

We have looked at the real-world problem-solving process and applied it to a problem of projectile trajectories. You should note that the mathematics presented are not that difficult. The important point to understand is that a specific procedure is followed in solving a problem. It's far more important to know how to solve a problem than knowing how to do the math (that's why we have computers). Recall that, in solving a problem, we should ask several questions. What's the problem? Can we solve the problem? How can we solve the problem? Does the answer we get make any sense? Is there more than one solution? What's the best solution? This is the problem-solving technique. I hope some of the math presented herein can be transferred to the classroom for practical exercises.

I'd suggest programming the equations on a calculator or within a spreadsheet. Then, for a given point (A, B), compute the minimum speed to reach that point. Specify a speed V, then determine the two angles that reach (A, B). Use this program as a platform for discussing the relative importance of each step of the outlined problem-solving process. After you try programming the equations on a calculator try some of these equations on a computer.

6. Another Look at Real-World Problem Solving

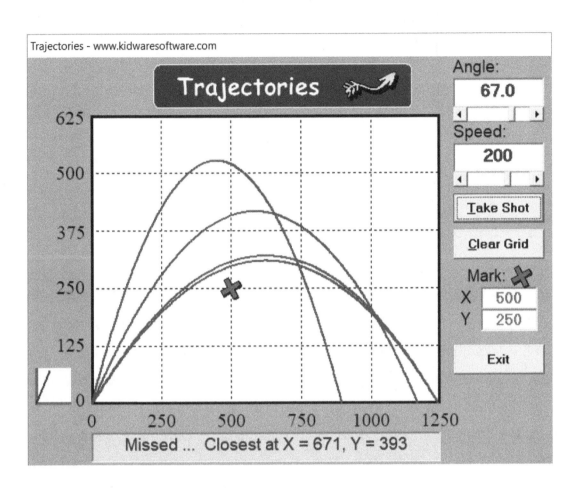

Introduction

In this chapter, the problem illustrated in Figure 1 was studied.

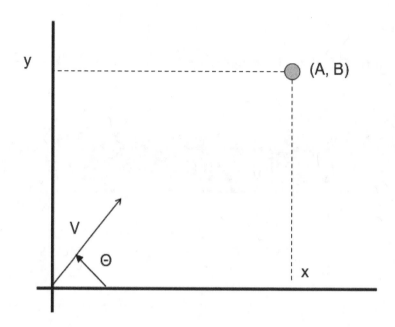

Figure 1.　　Projectile trajectory problem

This problem involves the trajectory of a projectile. The projectile starts its flight at the origin of the Cartesian (xy) plane with a speed of V at an angle of Θ. The problem is: we want the projectile to reach a desired point (A, B) by selecting V and Θ. In the previous work, a closed-form expression (an exact equation) for Θ, given a value for V and (A, B), was found. In fact, we found there were always two Θ values that reached (A, B). A closed-form solution was possible because of the relative simplicity of the inherent equations.

Closed-form solutions are rarely possible in the real-world. We usually resort to solving our problems numerically, using a computer. In this work, we look again at the projectile problem, but the solution emphasis is on iterative, numerical solutions. Both one-dimensional and two-dimensional solution methods are discussed, as are some of the checks that must be made and the pitfalls that should be avoided when using such methods. For classroom purposes, examples of potential applications of the trajectory equations are discussed.

Projectile Trajectories

For the projectile problem, we'll assume we know V, so we only need to determine Θ. The equations of motion for the projectile, ignoring winds, assuming only planar motion, and with gravitational acceleration (g) in the negative y direction are

$$x(t) = (V\cos\Theta)t$$
$$y(t) = (V\sin\Theta)t - \tfrac{1}{2}gt^2$$

This is our system model. With the desired (x, y) location being the point (A, B), we need to solve the equations

$$(V\cos\Theta)t = A$$
$$(V\sin\Theta)t - \tfrac{1}{2}gt2 = B$$

for two unknowns t (time of flight) and Θ (initial heading). In chapter 5, we eliminated t from the equations and found expressions for two angles that yielded the desired point. We repeat those expressions here

$$\Theta_1 = \tfrac{1}{2}[\sin^{-1}\{[B + g(A/V)^2]/(A^2 + B^2)^{1/2}\} - \tan^{-1}(-B/A)]$$
$$\Theta_2 = 90° - \Theta_1 - \tan^{-1}(-B/A)$$

Both Θ_1 and Θ_2 must lie within 0 and 90 degrees to be physically reasonable.

If V = 200 feet/second, g = 32.2 feet/second^2, A = 600 feet, B = 150 feet, the angles were found to be:

$$\Theta_1 = 29.68° \text{ and } \Theta_2 = 74.36°$$

The resulting trajectories are in Figure 2. We will use these solutions as a comparison basis for the two numerical solution procedures developed.

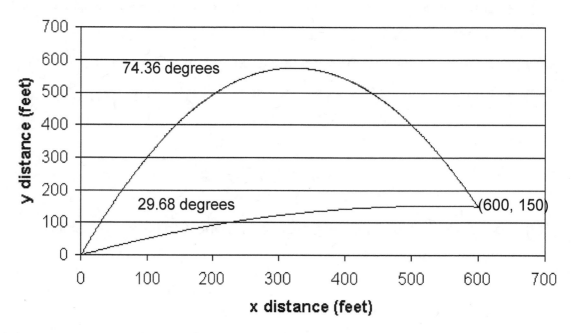

Figure 2.   Two trajectories to (600, 150)

We'll look at two procedures, one variable and two variable iterations. In each approach, we will need to make an estimate (guess) at what the solution is, see how well the guess works, and then refine our guess. This particular technique is called the shooting method because what we do is set our parameters, take a "shot," refine our parameters, take another "shot," and continue refining until we hit our target. (Just what was done in Lancelot's day using catapults - we haven't made a lot of progress since then!) Obviously, with a real system, we cannot physically make these shots - we'd waste a lot of equipment on our misses. So, in a missile (for example), the shots are taken on an onboard computer and once the proper answer is found, the real physical shot is taken. We'll do that here too - make guesses using the system model (x and y equations) until we find the desired answer.

One Variable Iterative Solution

In the first solution approach, we'll just work with one variable, Θ. We will assume a value for Θ and compute the resulting x and y. Based on how close these x and y values are to (A, B), we will then adjust Θ to try to get closer to the desired point. To obtain this one variable solution, we need to eliminate one variable (t) from the x and y equations. Note that once we assume a value for Θ, the x equation can be solved directly for t (time of flight) since we know V

$$t = A/V\cos\Theta$$

With this substitution, we will always end up at x = A. So, all we have to worry about now is whether y = B? Substituting t into the y equation provides

$$y = A\tan\Theta - \tfrac{1}{2}g[A/V\cos\Theta]^2$$

So, our solution procedure is: first, for a given Θ, compute y and see how close this is to B Then, adjust Θ to try to get a little closer to the correct y. Then, find y again and repeat the process until y does indeed equal (or is very close to) B Such a solution is called an iterative solution.

The big question is how do we use the computed y to adjust Θ so the next time y will be closer to B? One approach would be to just guess another Θ value and compute the associated y. Then, using interpolation (or extrapolation), find the Θ that would result in y = B. Since we are working with just one variable and computing a single result, this approach would work. In cases with several variables and many results, however, it would not work very well. In multi-variable cases, it would be difficult, if not impossible, to determine how much each individual variable change affected the final result(s). Without knowing such effects, we would not know which variable to adjust (and how much to adjust it) to allow convergence to the desired answer. So just guessing a solution is not the best general approach. Fortunately, we have the information we need to make an "educated" guess at the answer. Using the system model (x and y equations), we can determine the sensitivities of each computed variable to the adjustable variables. With these sensitivities, we can compute necessary adjustments to move closer to the desired solution. Let's see how to do this with our one variable solution.

It's easiest to illustrate the use of sensitivities for solution adjustments using a picture - look at Figure 3.

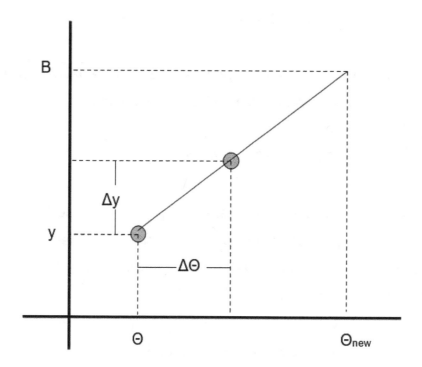

Figure 3. Solution sensitivities

Assume for our guess at Θ we have computed a distance y. We now want to know how much to change Θ so that the next y value will be closer to B. (If, with each adjustment, we move closer to B, we will eventually end up with the desired result of y = B). We need to know how "sensitive" y is to changes in Θ. To determine this sensitivity, let's perturb (change) Θ by an amount $\Delta\Theta$. Using this perturbed value of Θ, y changes by an amount Δy. Now, using the ratio $\Delta y/\Delta\Theta$ (the slope of the straight line in Figure 3, or the sensitivity of y to Θ), we compute in a linear fashion what Θ (we'll call it Θ_{new}) will give us y = B. From Figure 3, note B is described by the linear equation

$$B - Y = (\Delta y/\Delta\Theta)(\Theta_{new} - \Theta)$$

which is easily solved for the new Θ_{new} value

$$\Theta_{new} = \Theta + (B - y)/(\Delta y/\Delta\Theta)$$

This is our "educated" guess at what Θ will result in $y = B$. In this equation, we refer to the quantity $(B - y)$ as the miss distance. We want this distance to approach zero. The next step is to use this Θ to compute another y and repeat the above process until y does indeed equal (or is close enough to) B.

So, how do we find the key term, the sensitivity of y to Θ $(\Delta y/\Delta\Theta)$? We use the y equation

$$y = A\tan\Theta - \tfrac{1}{2}g[A/V\cos\Theta]^2$$

Recall V is known. The y from the above equation will be called the unperturbed y. Now, we perturb Θ by an amount $\Delta\Theta$. This yields the perturbed y

$$y + \Delta y = A\tan(\Theta + \Delta\Theta) - \tfrac{1}{2}g[A/V\cos(\Theta + \Delta\Theta)]^2$$

which yields

$$(\Delta y/\Delta\Theta) = [A\tan(\Theta+\Delta\Theta) - \tfrac{1}{2}g[A/V\cos(\Theta+\Delta\Theta)]^2 - y]/\Delta\Theta$$

We now everything we need to solve the problem.

In summary, the one variable solution procedure is:

1. Guess at Θ.
2. Compute y using Θ.
3. Replace Θ by Θ_{new}, as computed using the sensitivity factor.

4. Repeat process with the new Θ until B is reached.

Three quick points. First, I cannot overemphasize the importance of the initial guess at Θ. The guess must be reasonable or very strange results can be obtained. In this problem, we have a good idea of what to guess, but in many problems, much of the time involved in obtaining valid solutions is spent just coming up with reasonable first guesses. Some of the problems we solve in industry can involve thousands of variables that need first guesses! Secondly, you may ask why the iterations? Won't the corrected Θ we obtain drive us right to B the first time? After all, we computed the correction to eliminate the error in y. The answer is that we based the correction on an assumption that y varies linearly with Θ. Obviously, this is only an approximation, hence we only get close with our first correction - subsequent corrections get us closer. A last question to ask is: when does y equal B? In the real-world, equality rarely happens. Inadequacies in our system model, our measurement techniques, and other tolerances make it nearly impossible for one physical quantity to equal another. So we have to deal with the concept of "close enough." What close enough means depends on the problem and it is up to the person solving the problem to make this definition. In this problem, we say y is "close enough" to B when the absolute value *of* the error between the two quantities is less than 0.0005 feet. We also spend a lot *of* time in industry defining "close enough."

Now, let's look at the same example from our previous work (see Figure 2). Let's determine what Θ is needed to hit the Cartesian point (600, 150), assuming V = 200 feet/second. We'll assume a first guess of 45 degrees for Θ and when we perturb Θ to find the sensitivity factor, we will use a value of $\Delta\Theta = 1$ degree. (Another important point is how big and in what direction these perturbations should be. What is too small? What is too big? We won't worry about it here.) With these numbers, I obtained the following results (recall we are trying to reach y = B = 150 feet; the other point at x = A = 600 feet is accounted for in the sensitivity factor)

Iteration	Θ	y	$(\Delta y/\Delta\Theta)$	Θ_{new}

1	45.0000	310.1996	10.8386	30.2195
2	30.2195	155.4210	10.1029	29.6829
3	29.6824	150.0194	10.0775	29.6810
4	29.6810	150.0000	10.0775	N/A

The final answer is $\Theta = 29.68°$ (the corresponding time of flight is 3.45 seconds), which is one of the solutions we obtained with our closed-form expression. Note we obtained the proper solution quite quickly (only four iterations). Note, too, that the sensitivity factor ($\Delta y/\Delta \Theta$) is relatively constant. Many times, if this is the case, we can eliminate computing this factor at each iteration step and just leave it at its initial value. This reduces computation time and computer memory requirements which is often crucial if these calculations are being done on a small on-board computer. Let's check our answer for correctness. First, if we substitute $\Theta = 29.68$ degrees and t = 3.45 seconds back into our system equations, we do indeed find that x = A = 600 feet and y = B = 150 feet. That should give us a warm feeling. The answer seems reasonable also. Red lights and sirens should come on if your solution procedure yields $\Theta = -10$ degrees or 110 degrees.

Note this iterative technique converged to just one solution, yet we know there is another at 74.36°. If our initial guess at Θ is closer to this solution, would it converge there? Not necessarily so. Using this technique, if the initial Θ is between 1 and 62 degrees, the converged solution is 29.68°. If the initial Θ is between 63 and 67 degrees, the converged solution is around 209°, a non-acceptable answer - we're shooting backwards! This happens because, at these values, the sensitivity factor becomes small, causing numerical instabilities in the Θ adjustment. For initial guesses between 68 and 88 degrees, the procedure converges to the second answer at $\Theta = 74.36°$. Above 88 degrees, the large tangent values in the sensitivity factor begin to play havoc with the results and convergence is never reached. These results point out important considerations when using a numerical technique.

First, we again emphasize the importance of using an initial guess which is relatively close to the final answer. We see as long as the initial guess is close to an answer, convergence is reached. Secondly, we may not find all solutions to a problem. This may be because we didn't know there were multiple solutions or because there is not a one-to-one mapping of initial solution guesses to final converged answers. That is, some solutions may not be attainable with a simple shooting method approach.

Two Variable Iterative Solution

Solving the projectile problem is fairly easy because the x equation could be solved directly for t, making it a single variable problem. Many times, such direct solutions are not available, and we must solve multi-variable problems. Let's resolve this same problem as a two-variable problem, that is, we won't eliminate t from the solution process. The approach is the same, the mathematics a bit different and a bit more involved. We have the equations for x and y (our system model)

$$x(t) = (V\cos\Theta)t$$
$$y(t) = (V\sin\Theta)t - \tfrac{1}{2}gt^2$$

We have a desired point (A, B). We want to know what t and Θ values will allow us to reach this point. Our procedure:

1. Guess at t <u>and</u> Θ.
2. Compute x and y. Generate new t and Θ based on miss distances.
3. Repeat process, using new values in place of old, until we "converge."

The big problem is again finding how to adjust t and Θ, based on how far we are from the desired solution. We again use the idea of sensitivities and linear approximations. Following a procedure similar to that in the previous section, assume for a given t and Θ, we have a corresponding point (x, y). Define the following sensitivities:

S_{xt} - sensitivity of x to changes in t
S_{yt} - sensitivity of y to changes in t
$S_{x\Theta}$ - sensitivity of x to changes in Θ
$S_{y\Theta}$ - sensitivity of y to changes in Θ

If we know these sensitivities, we can write the following linear equations relating (A,

B) to new values for t and Θ (this procedure is analogous to that shown in Figure 3, where the sensitivities can be thought of as straight-line slopes):

$$A - x = S_{xt}(t_{new} - t) + S_{x\Theta}(\Theta_{new} - \Theta)$$
$$B - y = S_{yt}(t_{new} - t) + S_{y\Theta}(\Theta_{new} - \Theta)$$

In the one variable problem, it was a simple manipulation to find the adjusted Θ based on miss distance. Here, we must use Cramer's rule for linear algebraic equations. Solving these equations for the adjusted t and Θ values (t_{new} and Θ_{new}) yields

$$t_{new} = t + [S_{y\Theta}(A - x) - S_{x\Theta}(B - y)]/(S_{xt}S_{y\Theta} - S_{yt}S_{x\Theta})$$
$$\Theta_{new} = \Theta + [-S_{yt}(A - x) + S_{xt}(B - y)]/(S_{xt}S_{y\Theta} - S_{yt}S_{x\Theta})$$

Note that variable adjustments depend on both miss distances, (A - x) and (B - y). Now, let's find the sensitivity factors and then we can apply the solution procedure.

We want to know how "sensitive" x and y are to changes in both t and Θ. We need to find them in two steps. First, we hold Θ fixed, perturb t by an amount Δt and find the perturbed x and y values

$$x + \Delta x = (V\cos\Theta)(t + \Delta t)$$
$$y + \Delta y = (V\sin\Theta)(t + \Delta t) - \tfrac{1}{2}g(t + \Delta t)^2$$

These equations will provide us with S_{xt} and S_{yt}. These sensitivities are found by solving the first equation for Δx and the second for Δy and dividing both by Δt

$$S_{xt} = (\Delta x/\Delta t)|_{\Theta\ fixed}$$
$$S_{yt} = (\Delta y/\Delta t)|_{\Theta\ fixed}$$

Next, we return t to its unperturbed value, adjust Θ an amount ΔΘ and find the perturbed x and y values

$$x + \Delta x = [V\cos(\Theta + \Delta\Theta)]t$$

$$y + \Delta y = [V\sin(\Theta + \Delta\Theta)]t - \tfrac{1}{2}gt^2$$

These equations yield the other two sensitivities. If we solve the first equation for Δx and the second for Δy and divide both by $\Delta\Theta$, we obtain

$$S_{x\Theta} = (\Delta x/\Delta\Theta)|_{\text{t fixed}}$$

$$S_{y\Theta} = (\Delta y/\Delta\Theta)|_{\text{t fixed}}$$

We now have all the terms we need to attempt the two-variable solution. In summary, the approach is:

1. Guess at t and Θ.
2. Compute x and y.
3. Compute the sensitivities S_{xt}, S_{yt}, $S_{x\Theta}$, and $S_{y\Theta}$
4. Compute t_{new} and Θ_{new}. Replace t and Θ by these new values and repeat Steps 2 through 4.

The above procedure is repeated until the solution is "converged." It is up to the person solving the problem to decide when a solution is converged. Two criteria usually used are: (1) looking at how small the changes in the adjusted variables (t and Θ here) are becoming, and (2) seeing how close the solution is to the desired one.

Applying this procedure to the previous problem (V = 200 feet/second, A = 600 feet, B = 150 feet) yields the following iteration table. Initial guesses were Θ = 45 degrees and t = 2 seconds. Perturbation values of $\Delta\Theta$ = 1 degree and Δt = 0.1 seconds were used.

Θ	t	x	y	S_{xt}	S_{yt}	$S_{x\Theta}$	$S_{y\Theta}$
45.000	2.000	282.843	218.443	141.4	74.28	-4.98	4.89
13.698	3.141	610.241	-10.054	194.3	-56.50	-2.69	10.63
29.652	3.309	575.065	151.128	173.7	-10.33	-5.80	9.99
29.689	3.453	599.994	150.007	173.8	-14.88	-6.06	10.42
29.681	3.453	599.999	149.999	173.8	-14.89	-6.06	10.42
29.681	3.453	600.000	150.000	173.8	-14.89	-6.06	10.42

We get one of the same answers as before (Θ = 29.68°), so we must have done it correctly. Note here, it took a few more iterations which is expected since we are searching for two solutions, not just one. Also note the sensitivity factors here don't really stay constant until we get close to the solution, so we're probably better off computing them at each iteration rather than assuming they stay at their initial values.

Still, the solution converged to only one of the two possible answers. As seen earlier, the converged answer depends on the initial guesses at the answer. For example, if we begin the two-variable iterations with Θ = 45 degrees and change the initial time to t = 10 seconds, the procedure converges to a final answer of Θ = 74.36 degrees and t = 11.13 seconds. This is the other solution.

Concluding Remarks

By revisiting the projectile problem, we have seen some of the procedures of obtaining numerical solutions to real-world problems. Again, as before, we emphasize that the mathematics presented are not that difficult, though they may be tedious. The important point to understand is that a specific procedure is followed in solving a problem. And, in solving a problem, we should ask several questions. What's the problem? Can we solve the problem? How can we solve the problem? Does the answer we get make any sense? Is there more than one solution? What's the best solution? This is the problem-solving technique. Some of my ideas for possible use of this material follow.

First, the projectile problem is quite amenable to computer simulation. Programming the appropriate equations in a simple language like Visual Basic or Visual C# would be a good classroom exercise. Such simulations are very useful for 'what if?' type studies. Build in convergence checks, so the simulation knows when to stop.

The model used for the projectile is limited to xy motion and ignores wind. How would you modify the model to include 3-D effects and wind? What about height-variable gravity? This brings up another good point about problem solving. If you've written equations to describe the problem you are solving, you should always be aware that the answer you get is only as good as the assumptions behind the equations. For example, if you are shooting a projectile on a windy day, our "windless" model (even though the answers are mathematically and procedurally correct) would not be of much value. The model must match the real-world situation. You've seen this problem come up in Space Shuttle launches. Believe it or not, the Shuttle computers have a projectile model very similar to the one we developed here to compute its in-flight guidance corrections. Within that model are equations that describe the average wind conditions at Cape Canaveral on the day of launch. These winds vary with altitude. If, on the day of launch, the measured winds are not within some bounds of the average winds, the launch is scrubbed because the guidance corrections will be wrong, and the Shuttle will not go where it is supposed to. That's why you've seen launches canceled on days where it was too windy and also on days where the winds were not strong enough!

Discuss and study the importance of initial guesses for t and Θ. Using the two-variable method, try various combinations of initial conditions and see how the converged solutions change. Can you map out what values of t and Θ lead to which solution (in the case of multiple solutions)? Discuss and study convergence rates - is there any way to speed up convergence? Perhaps some modification to the linear variable adjustment schemes could be made. Discuss the relative merits of different criteria used to determine when a solution has converged. Two we looked at were insignificant changes in the adjusted variables and closeness of the solution to the desired point.

For the more adventurous, expand the dimension of the problem even more by making V (initial speed) a variable. I think you'll find this three-dimensional problem may result in many cases of multiple solutions. Such a problem will bring up another major consideration in real-world problem solving. What if your 3-D solution calls for an initial speed outside the realm of physical reality (for example, a speed larger than your projectile can provide)? Such a problem must be recast in what we call a constrained optimization. That is, find the "best" solution subject to physical constraints and restraints on the real system.

7. Solving Problems Numerically

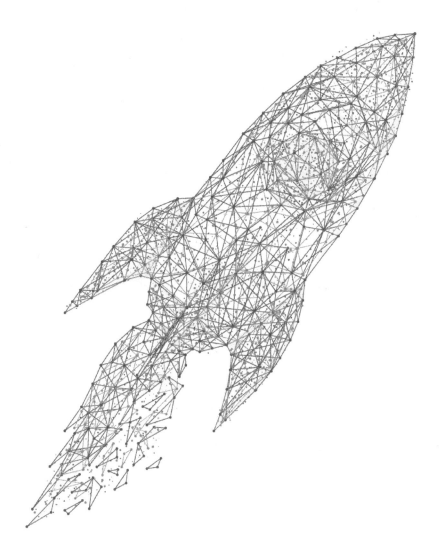

Introduction

Most classroom problems have closed-form solutions. That is, we can solve for the variable of interest and evaluate it (if necessary). In real-world problems, such closed-form solutions are usually not possible. The mathematics behind real problems are usually nonlinear and very complicated, which precludes direct solution. In real problems, we resort to numerical methods, solving the problems using a computer.

In this chapter, we look at solving two problems numerically. The problems solved are relatively simple and actually have closed-form solutions. We use simple examples to illustrate the steps involved in obtaining numerical solutions without getting too involved in the mathematics. And, by having closed-form, or exact, solutions available, it gives us something to check our real-world computer simulation software programming techniques. The first problem (one-dimensional) requires the determination of a model rocket engine's burn time in order to achieve a desired altitude. We include a Rocketry Simulation program in our Science Fair Software Suite of program to demonstrate this problem.

The second problem (two-dimensional) is a numerical implementation of converting from rectangular to polar coordinates. While solving these problems, we will address some of common problems encountered when implementing numerical (computer-based) solutions. Suggestions for using the example problems and potential expansions of the problems are addressed.

Model Rocket Launch

The first problem to be solved is illustrated in Figure 1.

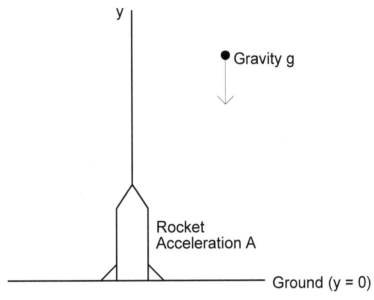

Figure 1.   Model rocket launch problem

We have built a model rocket and want to launch it. We want to determine how long the rocket engine should burn to achieve a certain altitude H by the time the engine burns out. While the engine is burning, the rocket generates an acceleration A (actually, the rocket generates a thrust, but Newton's law tells us the acceleration is that thrust divided by the rocket mass). Gravity works to counteract the rocket acceleration, hence the net acceleration (a) on the rocket during a burn is:

$$a = A - g$$

Note A must be greater than gravity (g) for the rocket to "lift-off." Under this constant acceleration, the vertical distance traveled by the rocket at time t is given by (just some simple physics - assuming zero speed at t = 0)

$$y(t) = \tfrac{1}{2}(A - g)t^2$$

And, if the burn lasts T units of time, the height at the end of the burn is:

$$y(T) = \tfrac{1}{2}(A - g)T^2$$

We want to know what value of T yields $y(T) = H$, the desired altitude. Wait a minute! If our desired value for $y(T)$ is H, it's pretty easy to solve this equation for T in terms of H - why do we want to use numerical methods? Mainly, to demonstrate the approach to numerical solutions. In most real problems, we can't write the equation(s) to be solved to in such a reasonable form - nonlinearities usually prevent such reductions. So, let's pursue the numerical solution, knowing we can easily obtain an exact solution to check our work.

To solve this problem numerically, we will use what the most-employed procedure in the industrial world is probably: we'll guess. Yes, we'll guess, but we'll make an educated guess and as we learn more about the problem, we'll make even better guesses. This guessing approach, sometimes called the "shooting method," involves making a guess at a problem's solution, seeing how well that guess satisfies the problem equations, and, based on that "closeness of satisfaction," make adjustments to the guessed solution. For our rocket problem, we will guess what burn time, T, will achieve some desired altitude, H. We will then use the equation describing altitude to compute what the altitude, y, corresponding to the guessed T value is. Based on the difference between the computed altitude and the desired value (H), we will then adjust our guess at T. We then compute the altitude corresponding to the new T and compare it to H. We repeat this procedure until the computed altitude is the same as the desired value H. Such a repetitive process is called an iterative procedure.

The big question is how do we use the computed y to adjust T so the next time y will be closer to H? One approach would be to just guess another T value and compute the associated y. Then, using interpolation (or extrapolation), find the T that would result in y = H. Since we are working with just one variable and computing a single result, this approach would work. In cases with several variables and many results, however, it would not work very well. In multi-variable cases, it would be difficult, if not impossible, to determine how much each individual variable change affected the final result(s). Without knowing such effects, we would not know which variable to adjust (and how much to adjust it) to allow convergence to the desired answer. So just guessing another solution is not the best general approach. Fortunately, we have the information we need to make an "educated" guess at the answer. Using the system model (the y equation here), we can determine the sensitivities of each computed variable to the adjustable variables. With these sensitivities, we can compute necessary adjustments to move closer to the desired solution. Let's see how to do this with our one variable solution.

It's easiest to illustrate the use of sensitivities for solution adjustments using a picture - look at Figure 2.

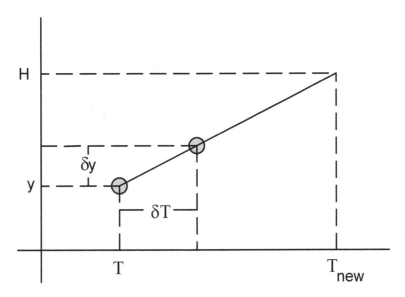

Figure 2. Solution sensitivities

Assume for our guess at T we have computed a distance y. We now want to know how much to change T so that the next y value will be closer to H. If, with each adjustment, we move closer to H, we will eventually end up with the desired result of y = H. We need to know how "sensitive" y is to changes in T. To determine this sensitivity, let's perturb (change) T by an amount δT. Using this perturbed value of T, y changes by an amount δy. Now, using the ratio $\delta y/\delta T$ (the slope of the straight line in Figure 2, or the sensitivity of y to T), we compute in a linear fashion what T (we'll call it T_{new}) will give us y = H. From Figure 2, note H is described by the linear equation

$$H - y = (\delta y/\delta T)(T_{new} - T)$$

which is easily solved for the new T value

$$T_{new} = T + (H - y)/(\delta y/\delta T)$$

This is our "educated" guess at what T will result in y = H. In this equation, we refer to the quantity (H - y) as the miss distance. We want this distance to approach zero. The next step is to use this T to compute another y and repeat the above process until y does indeed equal (or is close enough to) H.

So, how do we find the key term, the sensitivity of y to T ($\delta y/\delta T$)?. We use the y equation

$$y(T) = \tfrac{1}{2}(A - g)T^2$$

Recall A and g are known. The y from the above equation will be called the unperturbed y. Now, we perturb T by an amount δT. This yields the perturbed y

$$y + \delta y = \tfrac{1}{2}(A - g)(T + \delta T)^2$$

92

which yields

$$\delta y/\delta T = [\tfrac{1}{2}(A - g)(T + \delta T)^2 - y]/\delta T$$

We now everything we need to solve the problem.

In summary, the one variable solution procedure is:

1. Guess at T.
2. Compute y using T. Check to see if y = H. If not, continue.
3. Replace T by T_{new}, as computed using the sensitivity factor.
4. Repeat process with the new T until H is reached.

Three quick points. First, I cannot overemphasize the importance of the initial guess at T. The guess must be reasonable or very strange results can be obtained. In this problem, we have a good idea of what to guess, but in many problems, much of the time involved in obtaining valid solutions is spent just coming up with reasonable first guesses. Some of the problems we solve in industry can involve thousands of variables that need first guesses! Secondly, you may ask why the iterations? Won't the corrected T we obtain drive us right to y = H the first time? After all, we computed the correction to eliminate the error in y. The answer is that we based the correction on an assumption that y varies linearly with T. Obviously, this is only an approximation, hence we only get close with our first correction - subsequent corrections get us closer. A last question to ask is: when does y equal H? In the real-world, equality rarely happens. Inadequacies in our system model, our measurement techniques, and other tolerances make it nearly impossible for one physical quantity to equal another. So, we have to deal with the concept of "close enough." What close enough means depends on the problem and it is up to the person solving the problem to make this definition. In the example that follows, we say y is "close enough" to H when the absolute value of the error between the two quantities is less than 0.05 feet. We also spend a lot of time in industry defining "close enough."

Let's look at an example. Say our rocket can produce 100 feet/second^2 of acceleration, gravity (g) is 32.2 feet/second^2, and we want the rocket to reach an altitude of 2000 feet by burn-out. What should the burn time T (in seconds) be? We will use a value of $\delta T = 0.1$ second. With these numbers, I obtained the following results using an initial burn time guess of 4 seconds:

Iteration	T	y	$(\delta y)/(\delta T)$	T_{new}
1	4.00000	542.400	274.59	9.30828
2	9.30828	2937.235	634.49	7.83114
3	7.83114	2078.976	534.34	7.68334
4	7.68334	2001.242	524.32	7.68097
5	7.68097	2000.008		

The final answer is T = 7.681 seconds (check this answer using the actual y versus T expression - you should get the same number). Note we obtained the proper solution fairly quickly (five iterations). Now, let's look at solving a problem with two variables.

Rectangular-to-Polar Coordinates

The problem to be solved here is shown in Figure 3.

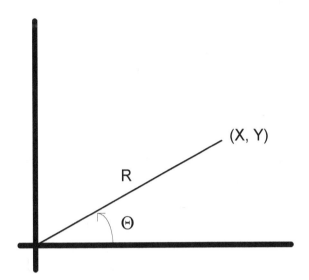

Figure 3.   Rectangular-to-polar coordinates problem

We have a point in two-dimensional space represented by the rectangular coordinates (X, Y). We want to determine the corresponding polar coordinate pair (R, Θ). We restrict the problem to positive values for both X and Y. The appropriate equations are

$$X = R\cos\Theta$$
$$Y = R\sin\Theta$$

We all know we can solve these nonlinear equations directly for (R, Θ), given (X, Y), but again we will use a numerical approach and use the exact result for checking our solution (if desired).

The numerical approach used here will be similar to that employed for the model rocket problem. Let's say our desired rectangular point is $(X, Y) = (A, B)$. We want to know what polar point (R, Θ) yields that coordinate. Our procedure:

1. Guess at R and Θ.
2. Compute X and Y. Check to see if $(X, Y) = (A, B)$. If not, continue.
3. Generate new R and Θ based on miss distances, $(A - X)$ and $(B - Y)$.
4. Repeat process, using new values in place of old, until we "converge."

The big problem is again finding how to adjust R and Θ, based on how far we are from the desired solution. We again use the idea of sensitivities and linear approximations. Following a procedure similar to that in the previous section, assume for a given R and Θ, we have a corresponding point (X, Y). Define the following sensitivities:

$$S_{XR} - \text{sensitivity of X to changes in R}$$
$$S_{YR} - \text{sensitivity of Y to changes in R}$$
$$S_{X\Theta} - \text{sensitivity of X to changes in } \Theta$$
$$S_{Y\Theta} - \text{sensitivity of Y to changes in } \Theta$$

If we know these sensitivities, we can write the following linear equations relating (A, B) to new values for R and Θ (this procedure is analogous to that shown in Figure 2, where the sensitivities can be thought of as straight line slopes):

$$A - X = S_{XR}(R_{new} - R) + S_{X\Theta}(\Theta_{new} - \Theta)$$
$$B - Y = S_{YR}(R_{new} - R) + S_{Y\Theta}(\Theta_{new} - \Theta)$$

In the one variable problem, it was a simple manipulation to find the adjustment based on miss distance. Here, we must use Cramer's rule for linear algebraic equations. Solving these equations for the adjusted R and Θ values (R_{new} and Θ_{new}) yields

$$R_{new} = R + [S_{Y\Theta}(A - X) - S_{X\Theta}(B - Y)]/(S_{XR}S_{Y\Theta} - S_{YR}S_{X\Theta})$$

$$\Theta_{new} = \Theta + [-S_{YR}(A - X) + S_{XR}(B - Y)]/(S_{XR}S_{Y\Theta} - S_{YR}S_{X\Theta})$$

Note that variable adjustments depend on both miss distances, $(A - X)$ and $(B - Y)$. Now, let's find the sensitivity factors and then we can apply the solution procedure.

We want to know how "sensitive" X and Y are to changes in both R and Θ. We need to find them in two steps. First, we hold Θ fixed, perturb R by an amount δR and find the perturbed X and Y values

$$X + \delta X = (R + \delta R)\cos\Theta$$

$$Y + \delta Y = (R + \delta R)\sin\Theta$$

These equations will provide us with S_{XR} and S_{YR}. These sensitivities are found by solving the first equation for δX and the second for δY and dividing both by δR

$$S_{XR} = (\delta X)/(\delta R)|\Theta_{fixed}$$

$$S_{YR} = (\delta Y)/(\delta R)|\Theta_{fixed}$$

Next, we return R to its unperturbed value, adjust Θ an amount $\delta\Theta$ and find the perturbed X and Y values

$$X + \delta X = R\cos(\Theta + \delta\Theta)$$

$$Y + \delta Y = R\sin(\Theta + \delta\Theta)$$

These equations yield the other two sensitivities. If we solve the first equation for δX and the second for δY and divide both by $\delta\Theta$, we obtain

$$S_{X\Theta} = (\delta X)/(\delta\Theta)|R_{fixed}$$

$$S_{Y\Theta} = (\delta Y)/(\delta\Theta)|R_{fixed}$$

We now have all the terms we need to attempt the two variable solution. In summary, the approach is:

1. Guess at R and Θ.
2. Compute X and Y. Check if (X, Y) = (A, B). If not, continue.
3. Compute the sensitivities S_{XR}, S_{YR}, $S_{X\Theta}$, and $S_{Y\Theta}$.
4. Compute R_{new} and Θ_{new}. Replace R and Θ by these new values and repeat Steps 2 through 4.

The above procedure is repeated until the solution is "converged." It is up to the person solving the problem to decide when a solution is converged. Two criteria usually used are: (1) looking at how small the changes in the adjusted variables (R and Θ here) are becoming, and (2) seeing how close the solution is to the desired one.

Let's try the approach with an example. We want to know what (R, Θ) corresponds to (X, Y) = (8, 2)? We will use an initial R guess of 5 and initial Θ of 45 degrees. Perturbation values will be $\delta R = 0.1$ and $\delta\Theta = 1$ degree. The corresponding iterations in the solution process are:

R	Θ	X	Y	S_{XR}	$S_{X\Theta}$	S_{YR}	$S_{Y\Theta}$
5.0000	45.0000	3.5355	3.5355	0.7071	-0.0622	0.7071	0.0612
7.0341	-3.6198	7.0200	-0.4441	0.9980	0.0067	-0.0631	0.1226
7.8796	16.7539	7.5451	2.2714	0.9576	-0.0408	0.2883	0.1313
8.2335	13.9107	7.9920	1.9794	0.9707	-0.0358	0.2404	0.1392
8.2463	14.0365	8.0001	2.0001	0.9701	-0.0361	0.2425	0.1393
8.2462	14.0363	8.0000	2.0000				

Six iterations are required to attain the desired result. You can check this result by back substitution into the original X and Y equations.

Concluding Remarks

We have looked at techniques for solving problems numerically. Though the example problems were relatively simple, the procedures developed could be applied to far more complicated problems. We follow a multi-step approach of guessing a solution, checking how close the result is to the desired answer, and, based on "miss distance," adjust our guess and iterate on the solution. What can you do with all of this? Some suggestions follow.

Play with the problems. Try finding different solutions. Study convergence to a solution as initial guesses are changed. What happens if you use "unreasonable" first guesses? How does the perturbation size (δT in rocket problem, δR and $\delta\Theta$ in coordinate problem) affect the convergence? What happens if you try to reach an impossible solution? Can you think of better ways to adjust the guessed answer? I'm sure you can find many interesting avenues to study with these numerical problem solutions.

Can you think of other problems that could be solved numerically? Try programming your own examples. Or, extend the two examples presented here. In the rocket example, the computed altitude is not the maximum altitude attained by the rocket. Once the burn ends, the rocket continues to climb (it has positive speed at this point) until gravity finally overcomes its upward flight. Can you extend the equations and solution to determine the burn time that results in a desired maximum altitude?

Another problem related to the rocket launch is sketched in Figure 4. In this trajectory problem, an object begins its flight (under the effects of gravity g) at the origin of the Cartesian (XY) plane with a known speed S at an angle of Θ degrees (measured from the x axis). The problem is to reach a desired point on the plane (marked by an X) by selecting Θ.

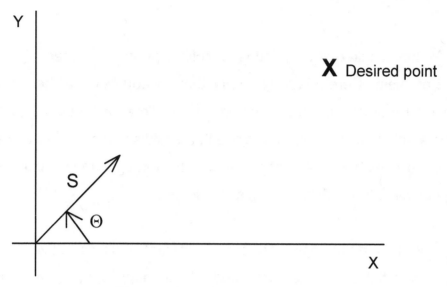

Figure 4.   Trajectory problem

The applicable equations are

$$X(t) = (S\cos\Theta)t$$
$$Y(t) = (S\sin\Theta)t - \tfrac{1}{2}gt^2$$

where t is time. If the desired point is (X, Y) = (A, B), we have two equations with two unknowns, t and Θ. Can you develop a solution procedure that computes what t and Θ result in the object hitting the desired point? Can you write a procedure that only requires finding Θ? Can you find an exact expression for Θ? In this problem, you must take care to insure you are trying to reach a viable solution. And another interesting thing about this problem is that there are usually two solutions for each desired point! How do you make sure you find them both?

An extension of the rectangular-to-polar coordinate conversion problem is sketched in Figure 5. This is a two-link robot arm.

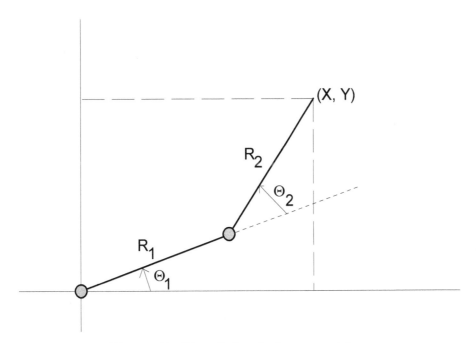

Figure 5. Two-link robot arm problem

Operation of the arm is simple. The first link (length R_1) pivots around the origin of an XY Cartesian coordinate system while the second link (length R_2) pivots about the connection between the two links. The two pivot points are drawn as circles. The angle the first link makes with the horizontal (X) axis is designated Θ_1, while the angle the second link makes with the first link is designated Θ_2. The end of the second link is the position of the robot arm, (X, Y). The problem is to find what angles yield a desired point (X, Y) = (A, B). The equations relating X and Y to Θ_1 and Θ_2 are

$$X = R_1\cos(\Theta_1) + R_2\cos(\Theta_1 + \Theta_2)$$
$$Y = R_1\sin(\Theta_1) + R_2\sin(\Theta_1 + \Theta_2)$$

Can you develop a numerical procedure that determines what Θ_1 and Θ_2 yield a specified rectangular position in the grid? Can your procedure handle both positive and negative values for X and Y? You should find two solutions for each point on the grid. Can you find an exact, closed-form solution for Θ_1 and Θ_2 (a difficult trigonometry problem)? Solution of this problem is central to robotics. In chapter 8, we will discuss in chapter 8, which will address these problems.

101

8. Mathematics of Robot Arms

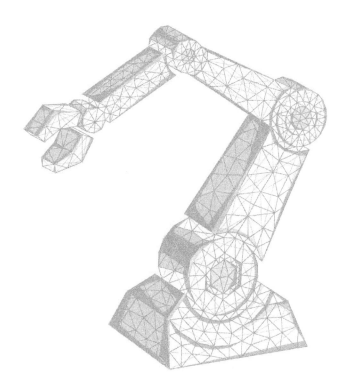

Introduction

Robotic arms are commonplace in today's world. They are used to weld automobile bodies, employed to locate merchandise in computerized warehouses, and used by the Space Shuttle to retrieve satellites from orbit. They are reliable and accurate. This reliability and accuracy are due to the computer a robot arm uses in determining where and how it should move. This control computer is programmed with some basic mathematics. In this paper, we will look at the mathematics behind robot arms.

We will study the two-link robot arm shown in Figure 1.

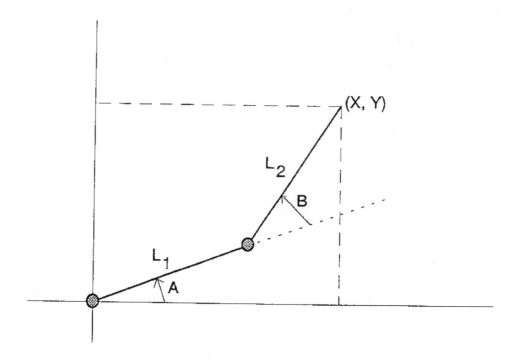

Figure 1.   Two-link robot arm

Most robot arms are more complicated than this, using three links and a moveable "hand," but with these complications come much more difficult mathematics. Operation of the two-link arm is simple. The first link (length L_1) pivots around the origin of an XY Cartesian coordinate system while the second link (length L_2) pivots about the connection between the two links. The two pivot points are drawn as circles. The angle the first link makes with the horizontal (X) axis is designated A, while the angle the second link makes with the first link is designated B. The end of the second link is the position of the robot arm, (X, Y).

There are three basic problems in robotics. The first problem is that of "kinematics." This problem asks the question: given the angles A and B, what is the arm position (X, Y)? This is simple trigonometry. The second problem is "inverse kinematics." Here, we want to ask: given the position (X, Y), what angles, A and B, yield this position? This is a more difficult problem. Lastly, we need to look at the problem of "trajectory planning." In trajectory planning, we ask: given our current position (X, Y) and some desired new position, how do we change the angles A and B to arrive at this new position? We examine each of these problems separately, using the two-link robot arm.

Robot Arm Kinematics

The kinematics problem requires computation of the robot arm Cartesian position (X, Y), knowing the two link angles, A and B. Referring to Figure 1, we can see the position of the end of the first link (X_1, Y_1) is given by

$$X_1 = L_1\cos(A)$$
$$Y_1 = L_1\sin(A)$$

Then, the end of the second link (X, Y) is simply

$$X = X_1 + L_2\cos(A + B)$$
$$Y = Y_1 + L_2\sin(A + B)$$

Combining these two sets of equations provides the solution to the kinematics problem:

$$X = L_1\cos(A) + L_2\cos(A + B)$$
$$Y = L_1\sin(A) + L_2\sin(A + B)$$

An interesting question at this point is: if we cycle A and B through all possible combinations (-180 degrees $\leq$ A $\leq$ 180 degrees, -180 degrees $\leq$ B $\leq$ 180 degrees), what would the region of coverage look like? If L_1 and L_2 are equal, the region would be a circle (radius $L_1 + L_2$). If L_1 and L_2 are not equal, the region would be annular (like a donut). This coverage region becomes important in the inverse kinematics problem, where we need to know if it's possible to reach a given point by adjusting the link angles.

Robot Arm Inverse Kinematics

The kinematics problem is seen to be fairly easy to solve. The inverse problem, that of finding A and B, knowing (X, Y) is not nearly as simple. Let's see why. Using the kinematics equations, if we know X and Y, we need to solve the following for A and B:

$$L_1\cos(A) + L_2\cos(A + B) = X$$
$$L_1\sin(A) + L_2\sin(A + B) = Y$$

This is a nonlinear problem. There are two possible solution approaches: algebraic and geometric. The algebraic approach (solving the equations directly) is tedious and involved. For the two-link robot arm, the geometric approach is more straightforward. We will outline the steps of the algebraic approach to illustrate some salient points of the inverse kinematics problem. Also, by outlining these steps, we allow the more industrious reader to see if he/she can solve the problem algebraically. After this outline, we will develop the solution to the problem with a geometric approach.

Algebraic Solution

In the algebraic solution, we first square both of the above equations and add them together. Then, we apply these trigonometric identities:

$$\cos(A + B) = \cos(A)\cos(B) - \sin(A)\sin(B)$$
$$\sin(A + B) = \cos(A)\sin(B) + \sin(A)\cos(B)$$
$$\sin^2(C) + \cos^2(C) = 1, \text{ where C is any angle}$$

Following these steps, we are able to obtain a relation for $\cos(B)$ simply in terms of X, Y, L_1, and L_2. That relation is (see if you can find it)

$$\cos(B) = (X^2 + Y^2 - L_1^2 - L_2^2)/2L_1L_2$$

With this, we can find B by applying the inverse cosine, or can we? What if $\cos(B)$ is greater than one or less than minus one? In these cases, there is no solution! When this happens, the desired point (X, Y) is not within the coverage region of the robot arm (as discussed in the previous section). If (X, Y) is in the coverage region, can we find a unique B? No, just knowing the cosine is not sufficient. If B is a solution to the above equation, so is -B since

$$\cos(B) = \cos(-B)$$

Hence, the inverse kinematics problem always has two solutions. This is shown in Figure 2.

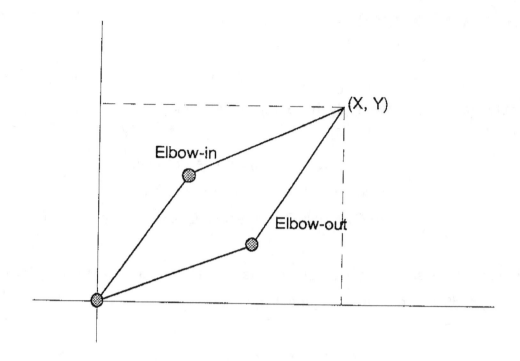

Figure 2.   Two solutions to robot inverse kinematics problem

In "robotics talk," one solution is referred to as "elbow-out" and one is "elbow-in." To specify which solution we want, we must also find the sine of B.

Knowing the cosine of B, the sine is given by

$$\sin(B) = \pm[1 - \cos^2(B)]^{1/2}$$

The angle B is then completely specified by selecting either a plus or minus sign in this expression. The robot designer must decide which sign to choose based on problem geometry and current arm configuration. This choice is discussed in detail in the "Trajectory Planning" section. Figure 3 shows the Cartesian quadrant in which an angle belongs based on the sign of the two trigonometric functions.

$180 > a > 90$ $\cos(a) < 0$ $\sin(a) > 0$	$90 > a > 0$ $\cos(a) > 0$ $\sin(a) > 0$
$-180 < a < -90$ $\cos(a) < 0$ $\sin(a) < 0$	$-90 < a < 0$ $\cos(a) > 0$ $\sin(a) < 0$

Figure 3.   Angle values in relation to sine and cosine

At this point in the algebraic solution process, we have the angle B. How do we find A? Knowing B, and hence sin(B) and cos(B), we substitute this (along with X and Y) back into the kinematics equations. Using the relations for the sine and cosine of the sum of two angles, the resulting equations will be (again, see if you can get these)

$$[L_1 + L_2\cos(B)]\cos(A) - L_2\sin(B)\sin(A) = X$$
$$L_2\sin(B)\cos(A) + [L_1 + L_2\cos(B)]\sin(A) = Y$$

Here, we have two linear equations with two unknowns: sin(A) and cos(A). Solving these equations (use Cramer's rule) and applying the angle convention in Figure 3 will yield a unique value for A. At this point, we have solved the inverse kinematics problem with an algebraic approach.

Geometric Solution

The geometric solution is more direct. We can develop expressions for the angles A and B by simply looking at the geometry of the problem. First, we'll find B. Figure 4 sketches the configuration necessary for this evaluation.

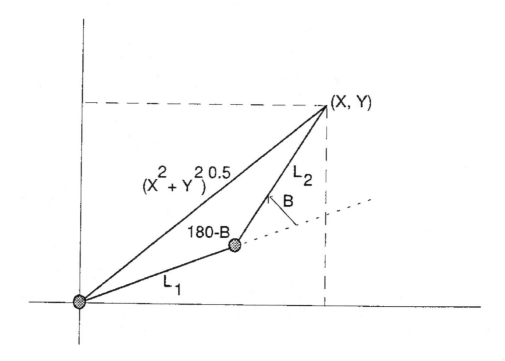

Figure 4.   Geometric solution for angle B

If we look at the triangle formed by the two links and the line [of length $(X^2 + Y^2)^{1/2}$] connecting the origin to the point (X, Y), we can use the law of cosines to write

$$X^2 + Y^2 = L_1^2 + L_2^2 - 2L_1L_2\cos(180° - B)$$

But, $\cos(180° - B) = -\cos(B)$. Substituting this into the equation and solving for $\cos(B)$ yields

$$\cos(B) = (X^2 + Y^2 - L_1^2 - L_2^2)/2L_1L_2$$

This is exactly the result obtained using the algebraic approach. The geometric approach is seen to be much simpler. Recall, though, that this does define a unique angle B. This definition is made by establishing a value for sin(B), as outlined in the algebraic approach.

The other angle, A, is found with a two step procedure. If we define the angle between link 1 and the line [length $(X^2 + Y^2)^{1/2}$] from (0, 0) to (X, Y) as C (see Figure 5), we can write

$$sin(C) = L_2 sin(B)/(X^2 + Y^2)^{1/2}$$
$$cos(C) = [L_1 + L_2 cos(B)]/(X^2 + Y^2)^{1/2}$$

These expressions define a unique C. Now, using the right triangle (Figure 5) defined by the three coordinates (0, 0), (X, 0), and (X, Y), we have

$$sin(A + C) = Y/(X^2 + Y^2)^{1/2}$$
$$cos(A + C) = X/(X^2 + Y^2)^{1/2}$$

which uniquely define A + C. Subtracting C from this sum will yield the angle A. This completes the geometric approach.

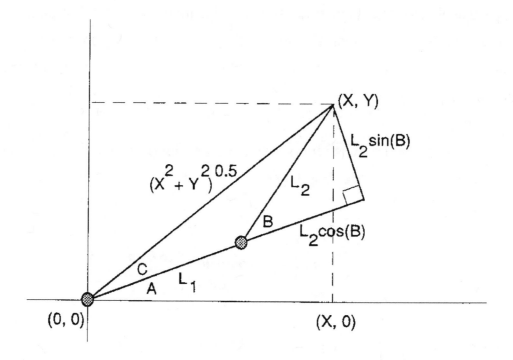

Figure 5.   Geometric solution for angle A

Robot Arm Trajectory Planning

The last robotics problem we need to solve is referred to as trajectory planning. Our two-link robot arm is at one position (X_{old}, Y_{old}), with corresponding link angles A_{old} and B_{old}. We want to move the arm to another point (X_{new}, Y_{new}). Assume we have solved the inverse kinematics problem and we know the angles, A_{new} and B_{new}, that correspond to (X_{new}, Y_{new}). We must decide how to change the old angles, A_{old} and B_{old}, so that they take on the new angle values. Do we change A first, B first, or both simultaneously? In which direction do we change them? Clockwise? Counterclockwise? This is not a difficult problem if there are no obstacles in the path of the robot arm, i.e. we have complete freedom of movement. In that case, we usually move A and B in the direction of smaller change. That way, we minimize the energy required to move the arm and the time required to change configuration.

As an example, look at Figure 6(a).

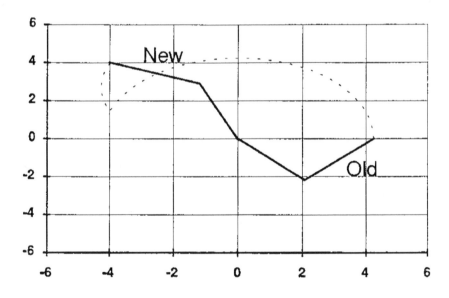

Figure 6(a). Trajectory from (4.24, 0) to (-4,4)

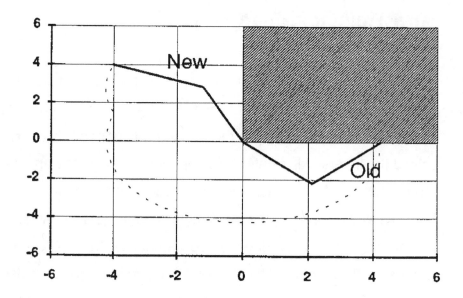

Figure 6(b). Alternate trajectory from (4.24, 0) to (-4,4)

Here, $L_1 = L_2 = 3$, A_{old} = -45 degrees, and B_{old} = 90 degrees, which corresponds to a Cartesian location of (X_{old}, Y_{old}) = (4.24, 0). Check the math using the kinematics equations. Say we want to move to (X_{new}, Y_{new}) = (-4, 4). To reach this point, the inverse kinematics equations yield A_{new} = 115 degrees, B_{new} = 39 degrees (see if you can get the same values - I have rounded to the nearest degree). We'll assume we can only change the angles one at a time. So, to go from (4.24, 0) to (-4, 4) with minimum angle change, we swing A from -45 to 115 degrees (counterclockwise) and then B from 90 degrees to 39 degrees (clockwise), as shown in Figure 6(a). What if there was a solid wall in the quadrant where X > 0 and Y > O? In that case, the trajectory in Figure 6(a) would not be possible? We need to change our plan. Figure 6(b) shows a trajectory that avoids the blocked quadrant. In this trajectory, A is changed in a clockwise direction. The two trajectories here achieve the desired condition, but not in the most direct fashion. We all know the shortest distance between two points is a straight line -let's see how to plan this trajectory.

To follow a straight line, we solve the inverse kinematics problem several times. We first draw a line from the current (X_{old}, Y_{old}) point to the new point. We

114

divide that line into some number of segments and compute the corresponding (X, Y) coordinates at the end of each segment using the equation of a straight line. For each (X, Y) pair, we compute the required angles, A and B, to achieve this point. As each new A and B is computed, we change the arm configuration. With this procedure, we move along the line until the desired endpoint is reached. The trajectory in Figure 7(a) shows the path followed by the example two-link robot arm using 20 intermediate points along the straight line (we have eliminated the blockage for now).

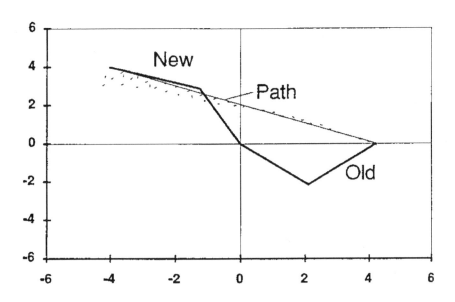

Figure 7(a). Straight line trajectory from (4.24, 0) to (-4, 4)

The path is not a straight line due to the nonlinearities of the robot arm and the motions as the angles are changed sequentially. If we changed the angles simultaneously, the path followed would be much smoother. We can extend this procedure to follow any desired trajectory. This allows us to get around any obstacles that might be in the way of the arm. Simply draw the desired path and compute Cartesian points along the path, along with the corresponding joint angles. Then, cycle through each pair of A and B values until the endpoint is reached. Figure

115

7(b) shows the arm following a three-segment straight line path from (4.24, 0) to (-4, 4). Again, this path would be smoother if the angles changed simultaneously.

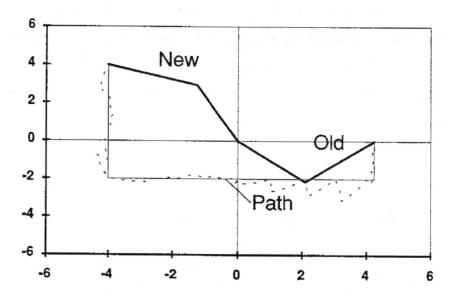

Figure 7(b). Alternate straight-line trajectory from (4.24,0) to (-4,4)

Obviously, there are many considerations in the trajectory planning problem. There is one last thing to discuss before moving on. Recall in solving the inverse kinematics problem, we need to choose B - whether we want an "elbow-in" or "elbow-out" configuration at each new point. The primary consideration in making this choice is potential obstacles, that is we must ensure the robot arm links do not collide with surrounding structures. If there are no potential collisions, we usually choose the B value that is closest to the current B

Concluding Remarks

The robot arm problem is a very interesting mathematical exercise. It represents nonlinear equations which may or may not have a solution. And, if a solution exists, there are multiple (two, in this case) solutions. And then, once the problem has been solved, many decisions must be made about how to implement the solution.

An obvious use for the equations as presented is to program them on a computer using a language such as Visual Basic or Java. Use graphics and allow the user to manipulate the angles A and B to watch the robot arm move. Allow for variable length links to investigate the potential coverage regions. Implement the inverse kinematics solution to allow for trajectory planning. Make sure you can detect solution existence. Determine methods of trajectory planning. Allow the angles to change one at a time or simultaneously. Can your robotic arm follow a straight line? Can you program it to follow any prescribed path? With such an implementation comes a question of resolution. In the discrete world of a computer, there are no two angles that will exactly correspond to some point (X, Y). However, there are angles that correspond "closely" to (X, Y). The robot designer has to decide what is close. If we can establish angles to within only 5 degrees, we have to allow for that sloppiness in our design. If we need more precision, we need to make it possible to have finer angle adjustments.

9. Fractals from Polynomial Solutions

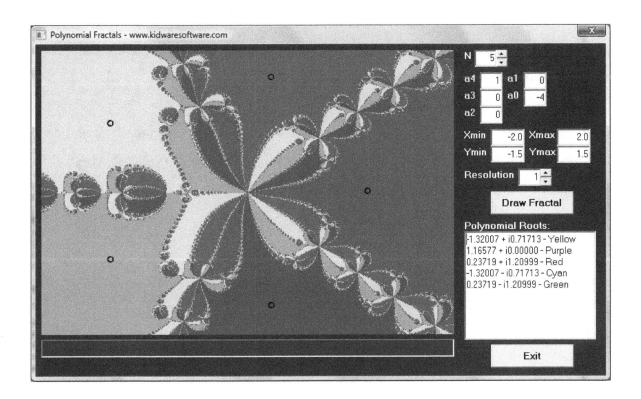

Introduction

Solving a linear algebraic equation is a simple process and to find the roots of a second-order polynomial, we use the quadratic equation. There are also specific procedures for finding the roots of a third-order polynomial. However, for fourth-order and higher, we need other ways to find roots. The usual approach is numerical. In general, for a polynomial of the form

$$f(z) = 0$$

we guess at the solution z and evaluate f(z). We then see how close we are to zero.
Based on the distance from zero, we make a refined guess at the solution and
continue until we have "converged" to a root, or solution.

A common algorithm for doing this solution adjustment is called the Newton-
Raphson technique (illustrated in Figure 1).

In this technique, if z_i is our current guess at a solution, we compute $f(z_i)$ and $f'(z_i)$
(the slope or derivative of the function). Our refined (or next) guess is where the
straight-line tangent to $f(z_i)$ at z_i crosses the z axis at $f(z_{i+1}) = 0$.

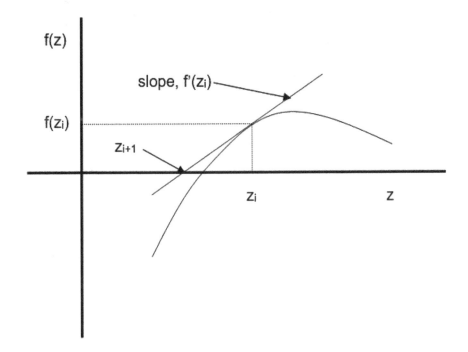

Figure 1.   Newton-Raphson solution technique

From Figure 1, we can write:

$$f(z_i) = f'(z_i)(z_i - z_{i+1})$$

Solving for the new guess, z_{i+1}, , we obtain:

$$z_{i+1} = z_i - f(z_i)/f'(z_i)$$

This is the primary equation of the Newton-Raphson technique. A major difficulty in using this technique is making sure we find all the roots. An nth-order polynomial has n roots. The Newton-Raphson technique will converge to just one root, depending on the initial guess at the root. We must find n different initial guesses that converge to the n different roots to completely solve an nth-order polynomial.

To use the Newton-Raphson method to find polynomial roots, we need an initial guess at a root, z_0. Every point in the complex plane (for high-order polynomials, it's hard to avoid complex roots) is a potential solution, hence a potential guess. If we use each point in the complex plane as an initial guess, compute the resulting converged root, and track which guess converged to which root, we obtain a mapping of initial guesses to final roots. This mapping, when drawn in color on a computer screen, can provide pretty and surprising results. Such mappings are fractals. We will develop a procedure for generating fractals from the solution of a general polynomial. For each step in the procedure, the pertinent equations are provided to help you understand the technique and develop your own computer routine (with modifications, if desired).

Roots of an nth-Order Polynomial

We will use the Newton-Raphson method to find the roots of a general nth-order polynomial of the form:

$$f(z) = z^n + a_{n-1}z^{n-1} + a_{n-2}z^{n-2} + \ldots + a_2z^2 + a_1z + a_0$$

where each a_i, $i = 0, \ldots, n - 1$, is a constant real value. The derivative (or slope) of this function is (you don't need to know where this comes from)

$$f'(z) = nz^{n-1} + (n - 1)a_{n-1}z^{n-2} + (n - 2)a_{n-2}z^{n-3} + \ldots + 2a_2z + a_1$$

We will use these two expressions in the Newton-Raphson equation to iterate on solutions for the roots. These iterations require complex arithmetic (complex in the sense we have real and imaginary parts for each number, not complex in the sense of being difficult), so you might want to review such operations. Each step of the solution procedure, and the subsequent drawing of fractals, is now covered in detail.

Search Region and Coordinate Systems

We can't search the entire complex plane for roots, so a first step is to determine the search region. We need to establish limits on the range of the initial guesses, z_0. Each z_0 has a real and imaginary part,

$$z_0 = x_0 + iy_0$$

[i is the square root of negative one (-1)] so equivalently, we need limits on x_0 and y_0. We assume x_0 can range from x_{min} to x_{max} and y_0 can range from y_{min} to y_{max}, or

$$x_0: \{x_{min}, x_{max}\}$$
$$y_0: \{y_{min}, y_{max}\}$$

The above limits cover an infinite number of potential initial guesses. How do we reduce this to a finite number? Fortunately, our desired display device, a computer monitor, has a finite number of points (pixels) for which solutions can be computed. So, we need to be able to convert a point on the screen (or some smaller display area on the screen) to the corresponding (x, y) pair in the complex plane. This is a straightforward process. Figure 2 relates screen display coordinates to complex coordinates.

Display coordinates are enclosed in square brackets, [c, r], where c is the display column and r is the display row. The upper left corner of the screen is [0, 0] while the lower right corner is [c_{max} - 1, r_{max} - 1], where c_{max} is the number of columns in the display and r_{max} is the number of display rows (meaning the screen is c_{max} pixels wide and r_{max} pixels high). Complex coordinates are enclosed in parentheses, (x, y). The upper left corner of the complex plane is (x_{min}, y_{max}) and the lower right corner is (x_{max}, y_{min}).

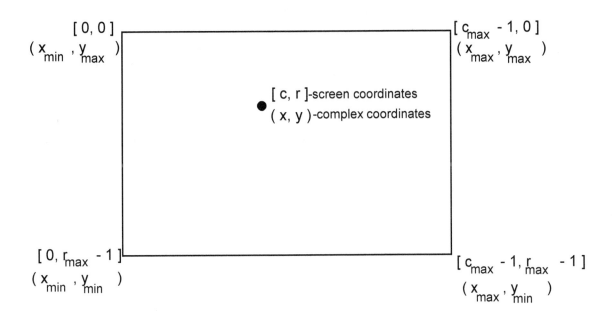

Figure 2.   Display (screen) and complex coordinates

Using Figure 2, we see that the point (x, y) is related to the screen coordinate $[c, r]$ by:

$$x = x_{min} + c(x_{max} - x_{min})/(c_{max} - 1)$$
$$y = y_{max} + r(y_{min} - y_{max})/(r_{max} - 1)$$

These two equations are different in form because of the way display coordinates are defined. Note x increases as the corresponding display coordinate c increases, yet y decreases as its corresponding display coordinate r increases.

Establish Initial Guess at Root

To draw the fractal representing the polynomial solution, we will assume every point on the defined display area is an initial guess at a root. Hence, we will systematically cycle through every point on the display, using the ranges:

$$c: \{0, c_{max} - 1\}$$

$$r: \{0, r_{max} - 1\}$$

This means we will look at c_{max} x r_{max} potential guesses.

Once we have selected the current screen coordinate [c, r], we use this to initialize our guess at a root. First, c and r are converted to the corresponding initial complex coordinates using the previously developed relations:

$$x_0 = x_{min} + c(x_{max} - x_{min})/(c_{max} - 1)$$
$$y_0 = y_{max} + r(y_{min} - y_{max})/(r_{max} - 1)$$

These values then establish the initial root guess, z_0:

$$z_0 = x_0 + iy_0$$

and we also initialize the iteration counter i at zero (i = 0).

Iterate on Root and Check for Convergence

At this point, we use the Newton-Raphson equation to compute updated estimates of the polynomial root. Recall this expression is:

$$z_{i+1} = z_i - f(z_i)/f'(z_i)$$

where

$$f(z) = z^n + a_{n-1}z^{n-1} + a_{n-2}z^{n-2} + \ldots + a_2z^2 + a_1z + a_0$$
$$f'(z) = nz^{n-1} + (n - 1)a_{n-1}z^{n-2} + (n - 2)a_{n-2}z^{n-3} + \ldots + 2a_2z + a_1$$

So, we use z_0 to compute z_1, z_1 to compute z_2, and so on. A few words on evaluating this expression. To compute a term like z_i^j, we multiply z_i by itself j times. In dividing $f(z_i)$ by $f'(z_i)$, if z_i is small, the denominator term may become very small and cause numerical problems - to remedy this, restrict the denominator to a minimum value (something close to machine precision). It is suggested that in all operations, the real and imaginary parts of the computations be kept separate.

After computing each new value for z, we must check for convergence, that is see if we have reached a root of our polynomial. A suggested convergence check is

$$|z_{i+1} - z_i| < e$$

where e is some small number. So, if our newly computed value has not changed much from the previous value, we assume we have reached a root, the Newton-Raphson iterations are stopped, and we color code the solution as described next. If convergence is not attained, we increment i and compute the next z value. In a computer implementation, it is suggested that convergence checks be made on both the real and imaginary parts of z. And, some limit on the number of allowed iterations should be in place.

Color Code Solution

Once we have converged to a root, we need to color code the corresponding display point (pixel) to indicate which root was reached. This is a relatively simple process. As each of the n roots is found, assign a distinct color to the root. Then, in subsequent calculations, determine which root the solution procedure converges to and color the corresponding pixel with the color assigned to that root.

Once we have colored each pixel on the computer display, the solution process is complete. At this point, a beautiful fractal will (or should appear). Let's look at a couple of examples.

Examples of Fractals

We'll look at fractals resulting from applying the solution procedure to two polynomials. The presented fractals were computed using the Fractals simulation program included in the \PolyFractals directory. The software is Microsoft Windows-based.

The installed program is entitled "Polynomial Fractals." In this program, you set the order of the polynomial (n) you want to solve (2 through 9). Then, you enter values for each a_i (i=0, …, n-1). You establish values for x_{min}, x_{max}, y_{min} and y_{max}. Lastly, you set a resolution value (1 through 10). This establishes the size of the 'dot' used to represent an initial root guess. For a resolution of 1, every dot in the fractal display area (over 240,000 points) will be individually colored. This results in a pretty plot but takes some time. Play around with different resolution values. In the code, onvergence checks are made with a value of e = 0.000001. Iterations are limited to a maximum of 1000 to avoid infinite loops. Once all values are set, you click the 'Draw Fractal' button. As each root is found, it is listed, along with the color used to represent it. A progress bar indicates how much time remains to see the fractal (low resolution values can take some time!).

Let's see a couple of examples. In each, a resolution of 1 was used. Figure 3 shows computed results for the 5th-order polynomial

$$f(z) = z^5 + z^4 - 4 = 0$$

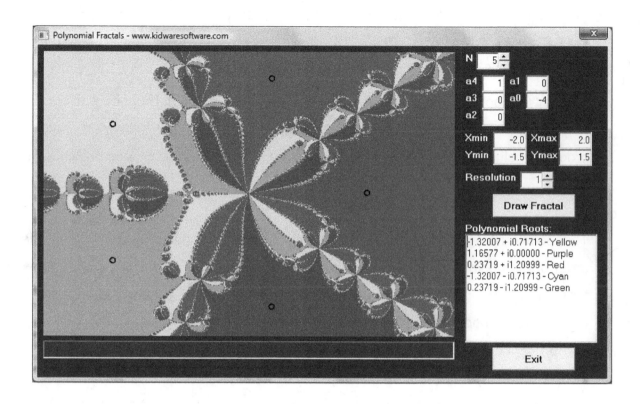

Figure 3.   Fractal for solution of: $z^5 + z^4 - 4 = 0$

(Polynomial roots are indicated by black circles)

Here, the range of initial root guesses was limited by $x_{max} = -x_{min} = 2.0$ and $y_{max} = -y_{min} = 1.5$. Notice how we set the needed inputs to the program. This polynomial has five roots, each marked by circles in the figure. We see that points around the roots tend to converge to the nearest root. Along lines separating roots however, there is some interesting behavior. Colorful patterns appear and guesses far from a particular root can still converge to that root. And slight changes in initial guesses can yield totally different results. These patterns are recognized as fractals.

Figure 4 shows similar behavior along boundary lines separating the nine roots of the polynomial

$$f(z) = z^9 + 8z^8 - z^7 + z^6 - z^5 + 3z^4 + 2z^3 - 5z^2 + 2z + 7 = 0$$

130

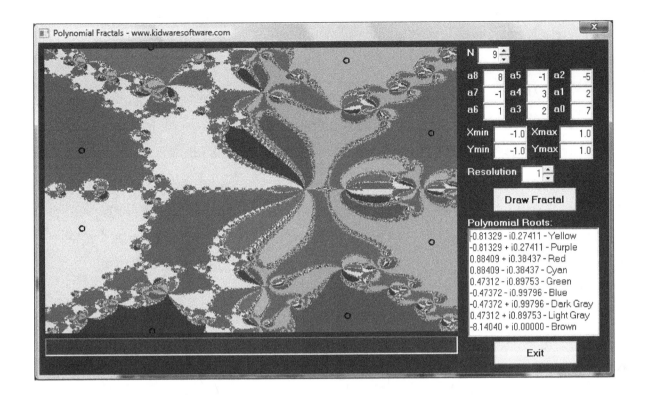

Figure 4.   Fractal for solution of:

$$z^9 + 8z^8 - z^7 + z^6 - z^5 + 3z^4 + 2z^3 - 5z^2 + 2z + 7 = 0$$

(Polynomial roots are indicated by black circles)

Here, the range of initial root guesses was limited by $x_{max} = -x_{min} = 1.0$ and $y_{max} = -y_{min} = 1.0$. Again, notice how the program inputs were set.

Concluding Remarks

We've looked at the behavior of the Newton-Raphson technique for finding polynomial roots and examined the mappings of initial guesses to final roots. We saw in Figures 3 and 4 that even if we make a first guess that is near a root, it is possible that the converged solution is at another root, far away from the initial guess. And, in the multi-colored regions of the fractals, we saw that the slightest change in an initial guess can result in a completely different converged solution! This behavior is a form of chaos, another interesting mathematics topic.

Though the solution procedure showed chaos, the resulting mappings seem to have some order (fractals). Now, we ask what good is all this? Well, it's fun to draw fractals and see that math can generate art.

10. Chaos in a Real System

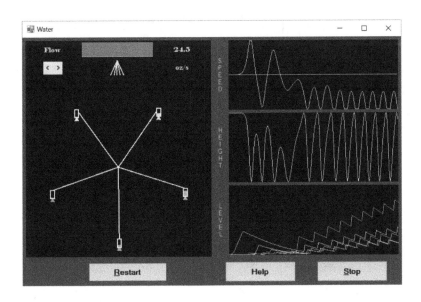

Introduction

The study of chaos began in earnest with Lorenz' weather models in the early 1960's. Most studies and demonstrations of chaos though usually address the behavior of simplified nonlinear equations as various parameters or initial conditions are changed. First-order population dynamics and Lorenz' third-order equations are classic examples of such simplified systems. This paper looks at a real dynamic system, based on first principles, and examines its potential for chaos. The system examined was first proposed by Lorenz as a mechanical analog to the convective heat flow that occurs as a fluid is heated from below. We'll refer to this analog system as the Lorenz water wheel.

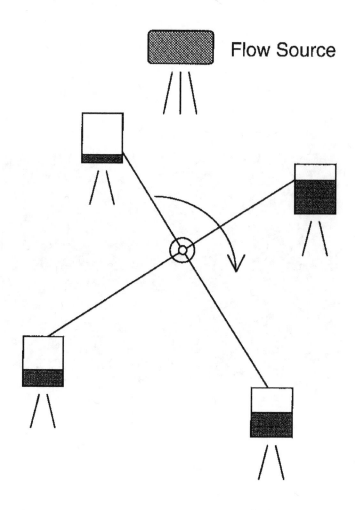

Figure 1.   Four bucket Lorenz water wheel

The Lorenz water wheel is shown in Figure 1. The wheel consists of two long spokes (perpendicular to each other) that rotate in a vertical plane about a center pivot. On both ends of each spoke are buckets (or cans) that can be filled with water. The weight of these buckets cause rotation of the spokes. A good mental picture of such a wheel would be a motor-less Ferris wheel with just four seats (one on each end of a spoke). The filling source is at the top of the wheel and as the buckets pass under the source they are filled with water. Each bucket has a hole in it, so the water is constantly draining, and refills are needed to maintain some rotation. If the source flow is slow, the top bucket never gets full enough to create a torque large enough to overcome friction and the wheel won't spin. Faster flows however result in heavier buckets which begin a rotation on the wheel. Certain flow rates may, in fact, create a steady rotation (as we would expect in a water wheel). Some flows can result in chaotic spins. The filling rates of buckets depend on how much time they spend under the filling source. If the wheel is spinning fast, the buckets will have little time to fill up. Also, if the wheel is spinning fast, heavier buckets will start up the other side before they have time to empty. Because of this, the buckets cause the spin to slow down. With such effects, the spin direction can actually reverse. In fact, the spin may reverse direction several times, never settling down to a steady rate, and never repeating itself.

In this work, we will model this four-bucket version of the Lorenz water wheel. Equations modeling the rotational dynamics, frictional effects, and bucket flow characteristics are developed. Then, implementation considerations for solving the equations are presented and some typical results presented.

Water Wheel Model

Modeling of the Lorenz water wheel is separated into three segments. We look at modeling the rotational dynamics, frictional effects, and the flow conservation within the individual buckets.

Rotational Dynamics

Figure 2 illustrates the terms needed to model the rotational dynamics of a four-bucket water wheel. The wheel is centered in a Cartesian coordinate system. There are four weight terms ($M_i g$, i = 1,2,3,4, where g is gravitational acceleration) at each end of the spoke, one for each bucket. Each spoke's length is L_s and spoke mass is M_s. We define Θ as the angle the arm of the spoke connected to Bucket 1 ($M_1 g$) makes with the horizontal axis. Each bucket acts through a moment arm to create torques.

135

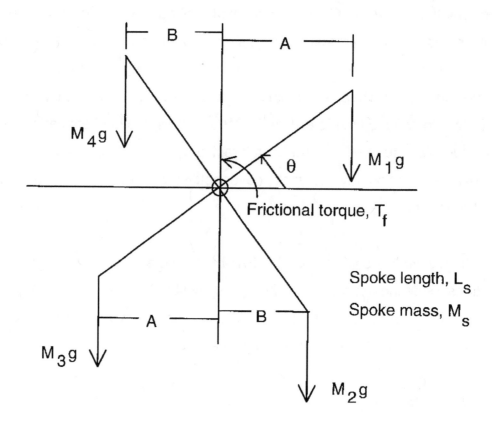

Figure 2.   Four bucket water wheel rotational model

Note the moment arms of Buckets 1 and 3 have a magnitude A, where

Equation (1): $A = \frac{1}{2}L_s\cos\Theta$

while Buckets 2 and 4 act through an identical moment arm of magnitude B

Equation (2): $B = \frac{1}{2}L_s\cos(\Theta - \pi/2)$

Note this choice of variables ensures proper signs on the torques created by the four buckets. A frictional torque, T_f, due to pivot friction is also present. Using the rotational form of Newton's equation and summing torques about the rotational pivot, we obtain the second-order differential equation (applying a right-hand rule for positive torques)

Equation (3): $J[d^2\Theta/dt^2] = -M_1gA - M_2gB + M_3gA + M_4gB + T_f$

where J is the overall rotational inertia. It is the inertia due to the spokes and due to the buckets on the ends of the spokes. The expression for J is

Equation (4): $J = [2M_s + 3(M_1 + M_2 + M_3 + M_4)]L_s^2/12$

(

Equation (3) models the second-order rotational dynamics. For simulation purposes, we like to work with first-order differential equations. We define two state variables, rotational position Θ and rotational speed $\dot{\Theta}$. With these states and Equations (1) through (3), it is simple to derive the two first-order state equations

Equation (5): $d\Theta/dt = \dot{\Theta}$

Equation (6): $d\dot{\Theta}/dt = [\frac{1}{2}gL_s\{\cos\Theta(-M_1 + M_3) + \cos(\Theta - \pi/2)(-M_2 + M_4)\} + T_f]/J$

Formulations for the mass terms are developed later. We now look at the frictional torque.

Rotational Friction

Friction in the water wheel's rotational pivot plays a key role in the chaotic dynamics. Figure 3 shows a section of the rotating spokes and illustrates the frictional effects.

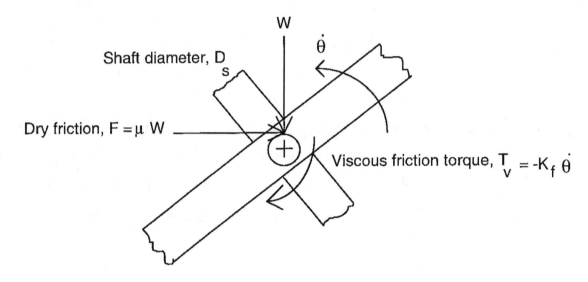

Figure 3.   Rotational friction model

There are two components to the friction: a dry friction and a viscous friction. We will look at these separately.

Dry friction creates a torque that depends on water wheel weight. The pivot shaft (diameter D_s) supports the weight of the entire water wheel which is the sum of the spoke and bucket weights:

Equation (7): $W = (2M_s + M_1 + M_2 + M_3 + M_4)g$

A portion of this weight is transferred, via friction, to a force tangential to the surface of the shaft. This tangential force causes a dry friction torque. Let's derive a relation for that torque. Assuming a coefficient of friction μ (0 to 1), the frictional force (F) is:

Equation (8): $F = \mu W$

The coefficient of friction depends on materials, lubrication, closeness of fit, etc. It is usually determined experimentally.

Note we must assign a direction to F. Friction always opposes motion; hence its direction depends on the rotational direction of the water wheel. Figure 3 illustrates the proper F direction for a counterclockwise ($\dot{\Theta} > 0$) rotation. With this expression for the frictional force, the dry friction torque (T_d) is simply force times moment arm (again, using a right-hand rule sign convention)

Equation (9): $T_d = -\frac{1}{2}FD_s, \quad \dot{\Theta} > 0$

If the wheel is rotating in a clockwise direction, the frictional force reverses direction, so in this case, the torque becomes positive

Equation (10): $T_d = \frac{1}{2}FD_s, \quad \dot{\Theta} < 0$

We can combine Equations (9) and (10) into one expression by using the **sgn** function. That is,

Equation (11): $\mathrm{sgn}(\dot{\Theta}) = \begin{cases} -1, & \text{if } \dot{\Theta} < 0 \\ 0, & \text{if } \dot{\Theta} = 0 \\ +1, & \text{if } \dot{\Theta} > 0 \end{cases}$

So, the dry frictional torque can be written as [using Equations (7) and (8)]

Equation (12): $T_d = -\frac{1}{2}\mathrm{sgn}(\dot{\Theta})\mu(2M_s + M_1 + M_2 + M_3 + M_4)gD_s$

This expression seems intuitively correct. If the wheel is spinning in a counterclockwise direction ($\dot{\Theta} > 0$), frictional torque is negative which tends to decrease $\dot{\Theta}$ (and hence Θ). Conversely, if the wheel is spinning in a clockwise direction ($\dot{\Theta} < 0$), frictional torque is positive which tends to increase Θ.

We assume the torque due to viscous friction (T_v) is proportional to the rotational speed of the wheel

Equation (13): $T_v = -K_f \dot{\Theta}$

The negative sign indicates the torque always opposes motion. The proportionality constant K_f (a friction coefficient) is a complicated function of the physics of the water wheel. An approximate expression for K_f is

Equation (14): $K_f = 2J\xi[g/L_s]^{1/2}$

where ξ is a viscous damping ratio ranging from 0 to 1. Experimental data usually determines a value for ξ.

Summing Equations (12) and (13) gives the frictional torque to be used in Equation (6)

Equation (15): $T_f = T_d + T_v$

So, now, we have expressions for the rotational dynamics of the wheel and the retarding effects of friction. The only terms remaining for consideration are the fluid flow characteristics of the buckets.

Bucket Masses

Figure 4 illustrates the terms required to perform a bucket mass balance.

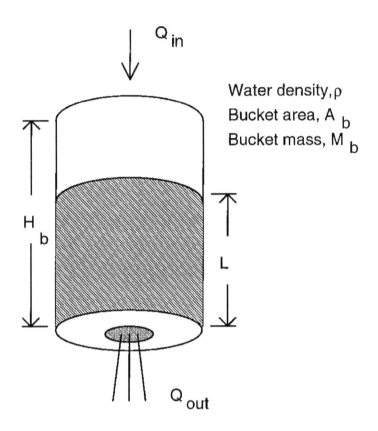

Figure 4.   Bucket mass balance

There are two components involved in finding the mass of each bucket on the water wheel. The first is simply the empty mass of the bucket (M_b) which we assume is the same for each bucket. The second component is the mass of the water within the bucket, which depends on how full the bucket is.

For bucket i, we can write its mass as

Equation (16): $M_i = M_b + \rho A_b L_i$, i = 1, 2, 3, 4

ρ is the density of water, A_b the cross-sectional area of the bucket (the buckets are assumed cylindrical and, again, each bucket is assumed to be the same), and L_i the level of water within bucket i. Each of the terms, except the level is assumed known and constant. The level depends on flows in (Q_{in}) and out (Q_{out}) of the bucket.

Performing a mass balance on bucket i yields the following differential equation

Equation (17):   Stored mass = $\rho A_b(dL_i/dt) = Q_{ini} - Q_{outi}$

which simply states the stored mass is equal to the flow in minus the flow out. The input flow exists only when the bucket is at the top of the water wheel under the input source. Rules checking for this condition are discussed in the implementation section. The output flow (due to leakage through the hole in the bottom of each bucket) is governed by Bernoulli's law which states the flow is proportional to the square root of the pressure difference across the hole, which is equivalent to stating it is proportional to the square root of the height of the water in the bucket

Equation (18): $Q_{outi} = K_h(L_i)^{1/2}$

K_h is a loss coefficient associated with the hole in the bottom of the bucket. This coefficient depends on the thickness of the hole, diameter of the hole, and material of the bucket. We can obtain an estimate of K_h for a real bucket by simply filling the bucket and then timing how long it takes to empty. Let's look at how that's done.

To empty the bucket, we have no flow in, so the bucket mass balance tells us (after substituting for Q_{outi})

Equation (19): $\rho A_b(dL_i/dt) = -K_h(L_i)^{1/2}$

If the bucket height is H_b and it takes t_e units of time to empty a full bucket, we can separate variables, integrate and solve for K_h. Or,

Equation (20):

$$\int_{Hb}^{0} Li^{1/2}\,dL = \int_{0}^{te} -(K_h/\rho A_b)\,dt$$

Doing this integration yields the following expression for K_h

Equation (21): $K_h = 2H_b^{1/2}\rho A_b/t_e$

    This completes the bucket flow dynamics. Note, we have added four first-order differential equations to the water wheel model. These four equations are [using Equations (17) and (18)]:

Equation (21): $dL_i/dt = [Q_{ini} - K_h(L_i)^{1/2}]/(\rho A_b)$, i = 1, 2, 3, 4

Implementation Considerations

We now look at how to use the water wheel equations in a simulation. We need to develop a procedure for computations, establish methods for integration, and determine some parameter values. Once this is done, we'll take a look at some typical results.

Computational Procedure

We have six state equations that need to be integrated: rotational position [Equation (5)], rotational speed [Equation (6)], and four bucket water levels [Equation (22)]. There are just a few steps involved in solving the equations.

We first need to determine each input flow, Q_{ini} for i = 1,2,3,4, that is we check to see if a bucket is "under" the flow source. Such a determination depends on the assumed width of the source. Figure 5 illustrates the particular technique used in this simulation (it assumes the flow source is at least as wide as a bucket). The top mid-point of bucket i (diameter D_b) is represented in Cartesian space by the point (x_i, y_i).

If the width of the source is W_s and the total source flow is Q_s (this should be a variable quantity to study chaotic motions), the input flow to bucket i can be written as

$$Q_{ini} = \begin{cases} 0, \text{ if } |x_i| > \tfrac{1}{2}(W_s + D_b), \ y_i > 0 \text{ or } y_i < 0 \\ [\tfrac{1}{2}(W_s + D_b) - |x_i|]Q_s/W_s, \text{ if } \tfrac{1}{2}(W_s + D_b) > |x_i| > \tfrac{1}{2}(W_s - D_b), \ y_i > 0 \\ D_b Q_s / W_s, \text{ if } |x_i| < \tfrac{1}{2}(W_s - D_b), \ y_i > 0 \end{cases}$$

144

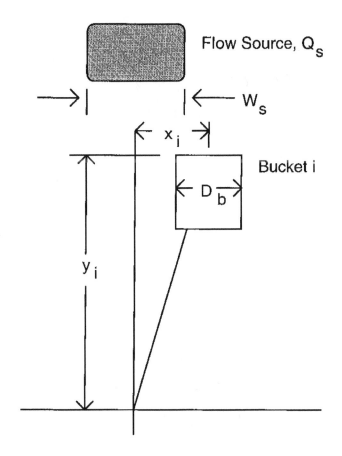

Figure 5. Bucket input flow determination

The relations in (23) simply express what proportion of the flow source is captured by a particular bucket.

Once input flows are established, we integrate the six state equations from the current state at time t, [Θ $\dot{\Theta}$ L_1 L_2 L_3 L_4]$_t$, to the next state at time t + Δt, [Θ $\dot{\Theta}$ L_1 L_2 L_3 L_4]$_{t+\Delta t}$. At this point, we save the variable information we desire and repeat the procedure.

A last computational consideration is initial conditions. We must ensure the water wheel system is initialized in a manner that allows the wheel to begin moving. First, the source flow (Q_s) must have a value. Next, we must assign initial values to each of the six states: initial wheel position, initial wheel speed, and initial bucket levels. Again, make sure an initial set is selected that allows for wheel motion. One

145

possible set is:

$$\Theta(0) = 2°$$
$$\dot{\Theta}(0) = 0$$
$$L_1(0) = 0$$
$$L_2(0) = 0$$
$$L_3(0) = 0$$
$$L_4(0) = 0$$

These conditions imply the wheel is not spinning and all buckets are empty. Bucket 4 is near the top of the wheel [$\Theta(0) = 2°$, see Figure 2]. With one bucket at the top and some initial source flow, that bucket will begin filling and eventually create a torque that begins motion. Note we cannot set $\Theta(0)$ to 0°, 90°, 180°, or -90°, that is have any bucket directly vertical. With such a positioning, the top bucket will fill, but there will be no moment arm about which to generate an accelerating torque.

Integration Method

There are many methods available for numerical integration. A goal in this work was to establish the simulation on a personal computer using relatively simple mathematics. To that end, simple first-order Euler integration was used and found to work satisfactorily.

Euler integration is a fixed time step method. For the water wheel, if we assume we know the state $[\Theta \ \dot{\Theta} \ L_1 \ L_2 \ L_3 \ L_4]$ at time t, the state at time $t + \Delta t$, (Δt is the integration time step) is

Equation (24): $\Theta(t + \Delta t) = \Theta(t) + \Delta t(d\Theta/dt)$

Equation (25): $\dot{\Theta}(t + \Delta t) = \dot{\Theta}(t) + \Delta t(d\dot{\Theta}/dt)$

Equation (26): $L_1(t + \Delta t) = L_1(t) + \Delta t(dL_1/dt)$

Equation (27): $L_2(t + \Delta t) = L_2(t) + \Delta t(dL_2/dt)$

Equation (28): $L_3(t + \Delta t) = L_3(t) + \Delta t(dL_3/dt)$

Equation (29): $L_4(t + \Delta t) = L_4(t) + \Delta t(dL_4/dt)$

where the derivatives in the above equations are found by evaluating Equations (5), (6), and (22) (for four buckets), respectively, at time t. When integrating these equations, you must look at some limits on the variables. It is first suggested that Θ be limited to values between -180 and 180 degrees. It makes plotting data a lot easier. And, note the four levels, L_1, L_2, L_3, and L_4, must always be within zero and the bucket height R_b.

Parameter Values

We're now ready to test the simulation. But we need real numbers to use in the equations. Presented here are one set of numbers (and the ones used to develop the results in the next section). You may choose any other numbers you prefer.

Physical constants are (using metric units)

$$\text{Water density, } \rho = 1 \text{ g/cm}^3$$
$$\text{Gravity, } g = 980 \text{ cm/s}^2$$

Selected spoke characteristics are:

Length, $L_s = 100$ cm

Mass, $M_s = 500$ g

Shaft diameter, $D_s = 1$ cm

Dry friction coefficient, $\mu = 0.2$

Viscous friction damping ratio, $\xi = 0.04$

The assumed bucket values are:

Height, $H_b = 15$ cm

Diameter, $D_b = 5$ cm

Mass, $M_b = 100$ g

Emptying time, $t_e = 60$ s

The input flow source (Q_s) was allowed to vary from 0 to 600 g/s maximum and assumed to have a width equal to twice the bucket diameter, $W_s = 2D_b$.

With the above selected parameter set, a time step of $\Delta t = 0.01$ seconds was used in the Euler integration and computation results were saved every ten integration steps. Let's look at how the wheel performs.

148

Results

Using the parameters just defined and the initial conditions discussed earlier, we can simulate the water wheel dynamics. For the cases presented here, the source flow was held constant at one-half the maximum, or 300 g/s.

Figure 6 plots the water wheel speed [with $\Theta(0) = 2°$] for the first 350 seconds.

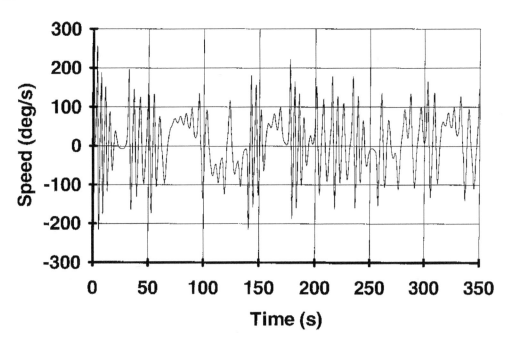

Figure 6.   Water wheel speed [$\Theta(0) = 2°$]

Recall a positive speed indicates a counterclockwise rotation. The wheel is seen to go through some initial starting transient, then tends to change rotation direction a few times. At around 70 seconds, the wheel seems to begin rotating steadily in the counterclockwise direction, but eventually deviates from this behavior and changes direction again. Note there seems to be no repeatable pattern in the speed response – this is the nature of chaotic systems.

Another characteristic seen in chaotic systems is sensitivity to initial conditions. Let's see what happens if we change the initial displacement a bit. Figure 7 is the speed response with all conditions the same except the initial displacement is halved to $\Theta(0) = 1°$. The wheel is seen to go through an initial transient and then go through several speed changes. After about 200 seconds, though, the wheel stops spinning! Now there's an unexpected behavior. What happened is the buckets of the wheel became balanced in weight and stopped in a position where the filling source was not above any of the buckets. A slight change in initial wheel configuration results in a drastically different response.

Figures 7 represent a response of the Lorenz water wheel. Many other responses are possible - that's what's intriguing about this system. There is an infinite variety of different responses possible, depending on flow rate and physical configuration. Investigating those possibilities is left as an exercise to the reader.

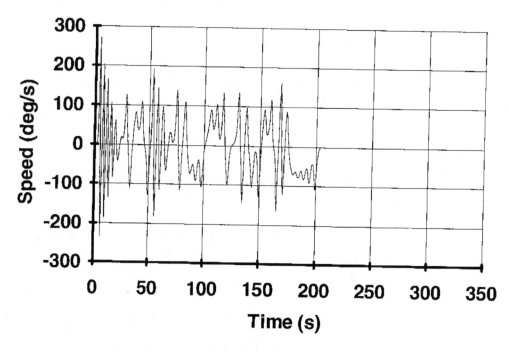

Figure 7.   Water wheel speed [$\Theta(0) = 1°$]

Concluding Remarks

Many demonstrations of chaos involve solving some mathematical equations that bear little or no resemblance to reality. In this paper, we have looked at a real chaotic system. We have developed the equations of motion for a four-bucket Lorenz water wheel and established procedures needed to simulate the dynamics.

The question is: what do you do with these equations? The obvious answer is to program them in some language and develop a simulation. Perhaps, add graphics to illustrate the water wheel motion. Make the simulation as general as possible to study the effect of changing physical parameters, initial conditions and input flows. Maybe make the number of buckets a variable. Or, make each bucket have different flow characteristics. Just play with the wheel. Can you ever get the wheel to spin at a constant rate for a long period of time, like a water wheel is supposed to work? Does plotting variables in the phase plane (speed versus position) result in Lorenz butterflies (see the reference book)? In working with high school students, I always suggest building a real water wheel and trying to see if reality can ever match the computer model. Try it.

Reference

Gleick, James, *Chaos: Making a New Science,* Penguin Books, 1987.

11. Computing Airplane Takeoff Speeds

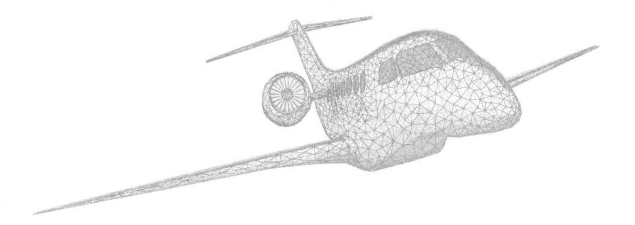

Introduction

This chapter describes the process performed by an onboard airplane computer in determining speeds the pilot uses in making decisions during takeoff. The mathematics involved requires knowledge of second-order polynomials, hence should be grasped by Grades 9 and up.

As a pilot accelerates from a stop, he/she must be cognizant of a quantity referred to as the decision speed. This is the speed at which the pilot must choose to either continue with the takeoff or abort the takeoff and stop the airplane. The value of this speed depends on many things: altitude, temperature, airplane configuration, weight, braking energy, and engine type, to name a few. But, for demonstration purposes, we can compute this speed using some simple physics and math. The speed can be determined in two ways: a direct solution and a numerical solution.

Problem Description

In computing the decision speed, we assume the worst, that is we say an engine (one engine on a two-engine aircraft, such as the Boeing 737, 767, 777) fails at some point in the takeoff, resulting in a sudden drop in acceleration. The speed of the aircraft at this assumed failure is the decision speed. The problem is: we need to find out how far in the takeoff procedure we can go, endure an engine failure, and still either takeoff safely or stop safely. To do this, we want to make sure the distance required to takeoff is equal to the distance required to stop. We call this the balanced field length solution. Let's look at how both the takeoff and stop distances are computed.

Takeoff Distance

The airplane begins its takeoff at a point we call brake release. At the decision speed, an engine fails, but the pilot continues the takeoff using only one engine. The time line for these events is:

where BR indicates brake release, D is the decision point, and TO is the takeoff point. (We assume we know the speed at the takeoff point. It is computed based on weather, altitude, airplane weight, and other factors.) From brake release to the decision point, we accelerate at a constant rate A_1 while from decision to takeoff, we accelerate at a rate A_2 (less than A_1 due to the engine failure).

The basic equations for speed (S) and distance (X) traveled over a segment of constant acceleration (A) are (think back to high school physics):

$$S(T) = S_0 + A(T - T_0)$$

$$X(T) = X_0 + S_0(T - T_0) + \tfrac{1}{2}A(T - T_0)^2$$

where T_0 is the time the segment begins, S_0 the speed at T_0, X_0 the distance traveled at T_0, and S(T) and X(T) are the speed and distance at time T, respectively. Let's write such equations for the two takeoff segments.

The first segment (brake release to decision point) starts at zero speed, zero distance, zero time, and has an acceleration A_1. So, for Segment 1:

$$S_1(T) = A_1T$$

$$X_1(T) = \tfrac{1}{2}A_1T^2$$

Let Segment 1 last T_D seconds (we don't know this value right now). At the end of the segment, we then have

$$S_1(T_D) = A_1T_D = S_D$$

$$X_1(T_D) = \tfrac{1}{2}A_1T_D^2$$

Note at T_D, the speed is set equal to the decision speed S_D.

Now, Segment 2 has an acceleration of A_2. It begins at T_D, has an initial speed of S_D, and an initial distance of $X_1(T_D)$

$$S_2(T) = S_D + A_2(T - T_D)$$

$$X_2(T) = X_1(T_D) + S_D(T - T_D) + \tfrac{1}{2}A_2(T - T_D)^2$$

This segment ends at T_{TO} (the takeoff time - again, we don't know what this value is) where

$$S_2(T_{TO}) = S_D + A_2(T_{TO} - T_D) = S_{TO}$$

$$X_2(T_{TO}) = X_1(T_D) + S_D(T_{TO} - T_D) + \tfrac{1}{2}A_2(T_{TO} - T_D)^2 = X_{TO}$$

Note, at the end of the segment, the speed is the takeoff speed (S_{TO}, a known value) and the distance traveled is the takeoff distance (X_{TO}). This is the distance we want to know. Let's rewrite the expression for X_{TO} solely in terms of one unknown, the decision speed (S_D).

From the expression for S_D at the end of Segment 1, we can solve for the decision time T_D

$$T_D = S_D/A_1$$

and from the expression for takeoff speed, we can solve for the time from decision to takeoff ($T_{TO} - T_D$)

$$T_{TO} - T_D = (S_{TO} - S_D)/A_2$$

Now, substituting these into the equation for takeoff distance (also using the expression for the distance at the end of Segment 1), it is left as an exercise for the reader to show:

$$X_{TO} = \tfrac{1}{2}A_1(S_D/A_1)^2 + S_D(S_{TO} - S_D)/A_2 + \tfrac{1}{2}A_2[(S_{TO} - S_D)/A_2]^2$$

So, to find the takeoff distance X_{TO}, we need A_1, A_2, S_{TO} (all assumed known) and the unknown decision speed S_D.

Stop Distance

In the stop assumption, the pilot accelerates to the decision point, then begins a deceleration, or stopping, procedure. The time line for stopping the airplane is

where BR indicates brake release, D is the decision point, and S is the point of zero speed (stopped). From brake release to the decision point, the segment is identical to that used in computing takeoff distance. From the decision point to S, we accelerate at a rate A_3 (a negative rate, so we slow down).

The equations for Segment 1 are the same as found for the takeoff segment. For Segment 3, the deceleration segment, the acceleration is A_3. It begins at T_D, has an initial speed of S_D, and an initial distance of $X_1(T_D)$. So, for this segment:

$$S_3(T) = S_D + A_3(T - T_D)$$

$$X_3(T) = X_1(TD) + S_D(T - T_D) + \tfrac{1}{2}A_3(T - T_D)^2$$

The segment ends at T_S (stop time), or

$$S_3(T_S) = S_D + A_3(T_S - T_D) = 0$$

$$X_3(T_S) = X_1(T_D) + S_D(T_S - T_D) + \tfrac{1}{2}A_3(T_S - T_D)^2 = X_S$$

Note, at the end of the segment, the airplane is stopped ($S_3 = 0$) and the distance traveled is the stop distance, X_S. This is the other distance we want to know. Using a procedure similar to that for the takeoff distance, we can obtain an expression for stop distance solely in terms of one unknown, S_D:

$$X_S = \tfrac{1}{2}A_1(S_D/A_1)^2 - \tfrac{1}{2}A_3(S_D/A_3)^2$$

So, we have expressions for the takeoff distance and stop distance written in terms of S_D, the desired decision speed. We can now solve for S_D. Let's look at two ways of doing this.

Direct Problem Solution

If we equate the two distances, we can directly solve for S_D in terms of the three known accelerations A_1, A_2, and A_3, and the known takeoff speed S_{TO}. This is just a messy manipulation of terms. When I did it, the result is (a good task for students)

$$S_D = [-A_3 S_{TO}^2/(A_2 - A_3)]^{\frac{1}{2}}$$

Note, this doesn't depend on A_1 since the distance traveled over Segment 1 is the same for takeoff and stop.

Let's try one case. Some reasonable numbers to use are:

A_1 = 6 mph/sec
A_2 = 3 mph/sec (½ of A_1 due to engine failure)
A_3 = -2 mph/sec (slowing the airplane down)
S_{TO} = 200 mph

With these numbers, I computed a decision speed of 126.5 mph. This means while the airplane is traveling less than 126.5 mph, it can still be stopped safely. Once the airplane is traveling faster than 126.5 mph, the airplane must take off.

Numerical Problem Solution

As formulated, we were able to find a solution to the takeoff decision speed problem. But unfortunately, in the real world, we can't always write such nice equations and find direct solutions. As you may have surmised, the equations above are gross approximations to the real takeoff problem. The real equations are extremely messy involving non-constant accelerations across segments, wind effects, and gross nonlinearities in the stop segment. And the actual equations are differential in nature (requiring calculus), as opposed to algebraic, all of which make it impossible to solve directly. Very few real problems have direct solutions.

To solve the real takeoff decision speed problem, we rely on numerical techniques. Simply stated, we guess at a solution (decision speed), compute the resulting takeoff and stop distances and see if they are equal. If they are, the guessed speed is the answer. If they are not equal, we adjust our guess and recompute the two distances. We repeat this procedure (iterate) until satisfactory convergence is attained. Even though we were able to obtain an exact solution for our simple problem, we can use it to demonstrate the iterative numerical technique.

Recall the takeoff and stop distances, respectively, are described by

$$X_{TO} = \tfrac{1}{2}A_1(S_D/A_1)^2 + S_D(S_{TO} - S_D)/A_2 + \tfrac{1}{2}A_2[(S_{TO} - S_D)/A_2]^2$$

$$X_S = \tfrac{1}{2}A_1(S_D/A_1)^2 - \tfrac{1}{2}A_3(S_D/A_3)^2$$

The solution procedure is, knowing A_1, A_2, A_3, and S_{TO}, guess at S_D. Compute X_{TO} and X_S. If equal, S_D is the answer. If not, re-guess.

Using a numerical procedure brings up many questions. First, how do you guess at an answer? Many times, this is one of the more difficult aspects of solving a problem numerically. You must make a reasonable guess, or your procedure may not work. In this problem, a reasonable guess is pretty easy - guess somewhere between stopped (S = 0) and the takeoff speed (S_{TO}). Secondly, once you guess at S_D and compute X_{TO} and X_S, how do you use the result to adjust your guess at S_D? Here, you must use your knowledge of the physics of the situation. That is, if X_{TO} is larger than X_S, which way do you adjust S_D to make X_{TO} smaller and X_S larger? Hint: the larger S_D is, the more room you need to stop the airplane. Lastly, when do you know you can stop the solution procedure? In reality, no value of S_D is going to result in exactly equal takeoff and stop distances. You must decide (using judgment) when the two distances are close enough. In the real program, if the two match within a foot, we say we are done, or converged.

Let's step through the numerical solution to the decision speed problem using the numbers from above. With these numbers, the takeoff and stop distances are

$$X_{TO} = \{3(S_D/6)^2 + S_D(200 - S_D)/3 + 1.5[(200 - S_D)/3]^2\}(5280/3600)$$

$$X_S = \{3(S_D/6)^2 + [S_D/(-2)]^2\}(5280/3600)$$

In these equations, the factor of 5280 converts miles to feet and the 3600 factor converts hours to seconds, hence the resulting distances are in feet. As a first guess, say S_D = 100 mph. With this, I find X_{TO} = 8555 feet and X_S = 4888 feet. We need to increase S_D to get a longer stop distance, X_S. How far do we increase it? Well, not past 200 mph! It wouldn't make sense to have a decision speed equal to the final takeoff speed. Try 150 mph - this yields X_{TO} = 7027 feet and X_S = 11000 feet. We went too far. Try 125 mph: XTO = 7868 feet and XS = 7838 feet. Closer. At 126.5 mph, X_{TO} = 7821 feet and X_S = 7823 feet. Pretty close. Note, fortunately, we obtained the same answer as that found with the direct solution.

Concluding Remarks

The takeoff decision speed problem is a good illustration of the application of some simple physics and some simple math. But, how can it be used for classroom purposes? I'll give you a few of my ideas.

With the direct solution, you could look at the sensitivity of the decision speed to the changeable parameters, namely the three accelerations (A_1, A_2, A_3) and the takeoff speed (S_{TO}). Plot the computed S_D versus these parameters. Can any trends be noted? Plot speeds and distances versus time for the various takeoff and stopping segments. Once you know S_D, compute the required runway length. A tricky problem is: given a known runway length, can you find a set of parameters that uses the entire runway for a takeoff or stop? That brings up another question. What if the takeoff (or stop) distance resulting from a given decision speed computation is longer than the runway? What can you do? This is a common problem at some airports.

The numerical solution points out some of the difficulties in solving real problems. How do you find a first guess? How do you adjust your guess knowing some intermediate solution? And, how do you know when you are done solving the problem? These are all very important considerations when attacking real math problems. A final point we didn't look at that can really cause havoc is the area of multiple solutions. Many problems have more than one solution - how do you determine if you have found the solution that meets your needs in the best way? That topic is an article by itself. As an example, note our decision speed example actually has another solution at -126.5 mph, but very few airplanes can takeoff when flying backwards!

Many things can be tried with the numerical solution. As described, the current solution process is inflexible. It assumes two constant acceleration segments in both the takeoff and stopping legs. If any of these assumptions were to change, we would have to derive new expressions for takeoff and stopping distances. To enhance the flexibility of the solution procedure, a first suggestion would be to program the equations on a computer and develop your own solution procedure. Doing this gives you a lot of flexibility in trying new things. For example, it would be easy to add a third segment to the takeoff or stopping procedure. Using a computer program opens up many avenues for further study. Our company offers several programming tutorials (Visual Basic, Small Basic, C#, Java) that provide the skills to build such a program – see our website for details.

Implement an automatic solution adjustment procedure. Note that the stop distance is far more sensitive to changes in S_D than the takeoff distance - we can use that fact in our adjustment algorithm. One approach is, for each guessed S_D, plot the resulting X_{TO} and X_S, then use linear interpolation to obtain a next guess for S_D. This chart shows such a procedure for the numerical example we used previously.

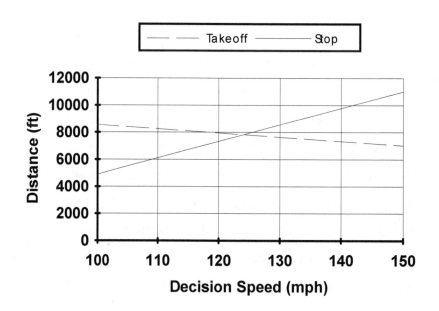

Recall at 100 mph, X_{TO} = 8555 feet and X_S = 4888 feet, while at 150 mph, X_{TO} = 7027 feet and X_S = 11000 feet. The intersection of these lines shows where X_{TO} = X_S. From the graph, we find the corresponding speed is about S_D = 124 mph. This would be our next guess at S_D, and then interpolation would again be used to find a new S_D. Such adjustments are continued until the takeoff and stop distances are equal (or at least close enough). It should be simple to program such a procedure. You may wonder why the first correction does not yield the correct answer of 126.5 mph. You might ask your students this. It has to do with the fact that the distances are not linear functions of speed.

Similar to what could be done with the direct solution procedure, you could use your programmed solution to investigate sensitivities to assumed parameters or to determine necessary accelerations and takeoff speed (S_{TO}) to meet some other specifications. If you are really adventurous, here's a challenge. In the real onboard computer program, we do not obtain a solution by varying the decision speed. Instead, we vary the time of decision (T_D). The reasons for this are many, but the main reason is that it gives us a more tractable and flexible solution. I'll outline the procedure using the equations developed here. See if you (or your students) can program it.

To minimize looking back at previous results, I'll repeat any needed equations. The goal here is the same: find the decision speed (S_D) that results in equal takeoff (X_{TO}) and stopping (X_S) distances. The procedure is just different.

The steps are:

1. Guess at the time of decision (T_D). Compute speed and distance at T_D (Segment 1)

$$S_1 = A_1 T_D$$
$$X_1 = \tfrac{1}{2} A_1 T_D^2$$

2. Compute the time of takeoff (T_{TO}) using the known takeoff speed (S_{TO})

$$T_{TO} = T_D + (S_{TO} - S_1)/A_2$$

A quick note. In the actual program, we must guess at T_{TO} because Segment 2 is not a constant acceleration segment. With our guessed value, we then compute the speed at T_{TO}. If this speed matches S_{TO}, we continue. If not, we have to adjust our guess at T_{TO} to move the computed speed closer to the desired value. The adjustment procedure is similar to that outlined previously for the decision speed, i.e. we use linear interpolation.

3. Compute the takeoff distance (Segment 2)

$$X_{TO} = X_1 + S_1(T_{TO} - T_D) + \tfrac{1}{2} A_2 (T_{TO} - T_D)^2$$

4. Begin stop calculations. Compute the time at which the airplane is stopped (T_S)

$$T_S = T_D - S_1/A_3$$

Again, in the real program, we must guess at T_S and perform adjustments until the speed at the end of Segment 3 is zero (or at least close to zero).

4. Compute the stop distance (Segment 3)

$$X_S = X_1 + S_1(T_S - T_D) + \tfrac{1}{2}A_3(T_S - T_D)^2$$

5. Compare the takeoff and stop distances. If equal, set $S_D = S_1$ (computed in Step 1, the speed at the end of Segment 1) and stop the procedure. If not equal, adjust T_D using an appropriate algorithm and repeat Steps 1 through 5.

A last suggestion would be to actually program a procedure for iterating on values for T_{TO} (takeoff time) and T_S (stop time), instead of computing them directly. This would yield added flexibility to the program. And students would have to decide on methods for adjusting their guesses based on computed speeds.

To get you started on calculating Polynomials we have included our Polynomial Equation Software program in this directory.

12. Computing Airplane Stopping Distance

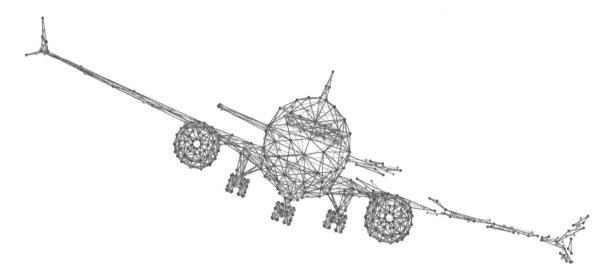

Introduction

In beginning calculus courses, it is often helpful to have real-world applications that use derivatives. This article presents two such applications related to computing the distance required to stop an airplane. This is an important problem because this distance must be within the constraints of the runways where a plane might land.

The basic equation used to compute the stopping distance for an airplane is Newton's law, F = ma. That is, the sum of the forces acting on the plane is equal to the product of its mass and acceleration. So, if we know the forces acting on the plane and its mass, we can solve for the acceleration (actually a deceleration when stopping). Knowing the deceleration, we can determine the airplane speed and distance traveled while stopping. The key here is to determine the forces acting on the airplane while it is stopping. There are three major forces acting on an airplane while it stops. First, the pilot can reverse the thrust on the engines to slow the plane (we'll ignore this here). Following touchdown, the pilot cuts the engine throttles and applies a set of brakes very similar to those used in automobiles. This braking force

169

and aerodynamic drag (friction) are the other two forces that contribute to deceleration. To compute the deceleration and stopping distance, we need mathematical descriptions of how the brake force and aerodynamic drag change over time. This chapter develops such descriptions and shows how they are used to compute stopping distance.

Two problems are studied. First, we look at using curve-fitting techniques to develop an equation for brake force that insures a smooth transition from zero braking to full braking force. Second, we develop equations for the deceleration and speed of an airplane and show how we can numerically solve these equations (simple differential equations) to obtain an approximate value for stopping distance. Example data and results are presented for several different airplane models.

Problem 1 - Braking Force

Figure 1 illustrates the braking problem we need to solve.

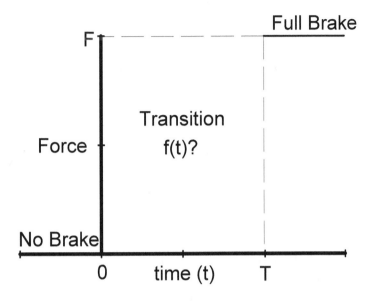

Figure 1. Airplane braking force

Segments of the braking force are plotted as a function of time (t). We assume the pilot applies the brakes at time zero (t = 0). Up to this time, the braking force is zero. It takes T seconds to reach full braking force F, and after this time, the full braking force is maintained. But, how do we describe the braking force as it transitions from zero to F? We will define this force change by the function f(t).

One possible solution is shown in Figure 2. Here, we simply connect a straight line between the points (0, 0) and (T, F). The equation for f(t) is then

$$\text{Force} = f(t) = F(t/T), \ 0 \le t \le T$$

This line meets the requirements that at t = 0, there is zero force and at t = T, the braking force is F. But there is one major problem with using a straight line. Because of the sharp corners on the force curve at t = 0 and t = T, the derivative of

171

the braking force does not exist at these points. This presents a difficulty. Most techniques used in solving real-world problems require smooth curves with existing derivatives. Hence, the straight-line approximation of Figure 2 may make it difficult to solve the stopping problem. We need another description for the braking force.

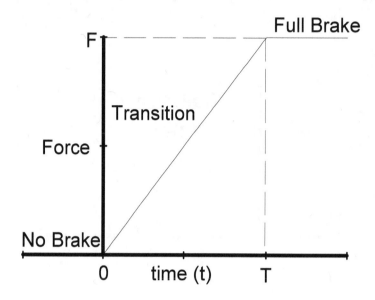

Figure 2. Straight-line braking force function

Before going on, let's look a little closer at the straight line description. You may be asking: how can you say that a derivative does not exist? It's easy to see that f(t) has a derivative

$$f'(t) = F/T, \text{ when } 0 \le t \le T$$

The above relation is true, and at both t = 0 and t = T, the derivative is F/T. The question of derivative existence arises when looking at the derivatives of braking force prior to brake application and following full braking force. Since the force is constant in these periods, the force derivative is zero. This conflicts with the derivative value (F/T) derived from the transitional force. The derivatives do not match at t = 0 and t = T, hence the derivative does not exist at these points. It does,

172

however, exist at all other points in time. So, what we need is an alternate description of the transitional brake force, f(t), where not only does the force match at t = 0 and t = T, but also the derivatives. That description is developed next.

We need a transitional brake force description, f(t), where

$$f(0) = 0 \text{ and } f(T) = F$$

and where the derivative, f'(t), exists and is zero-valued (recall that prior to brake application and at full brake condition, the brake force is a constant with zero derivative) at t = 0 and t = T. We need a function f(t) that matches the four specified conditions. In reality, there are an infinite number of functions that match these conditions (can you find some of them?). We will choose one of the simplest functions, a polynomial in time.

Since there are four end conditions to match, our polynomial will need at least four coefficients. This corresponds most simply to a third-order polynomial. Thus, the proposed braking force equation has the form

$$f(t) = a_0 + a_1 t + a_2 t^2 + a_3 t^3, \; 0 \le t \le T$$

where the coefficients a_0, a_1, a_2, and a_3 will be determined by applying the specified end conditions. [Note this force is only valid from t = 0 to t = T (it cannot be used outside these time values)]. The derivative of f(t) is

$$f'(t) = a_1 + 2a_2 t + 3a_3 t^2, \; 0 \le t \le T$$

To find the coefficients, first match the braking force and its derivative at t = 0:

173

$$f(0) = a_0 = 0$$

$$f'(0) = a_1 = 0$$

With these two coefficients (a_0 and a_1) equal to zero, the braking force and its derivative are now given by:

$$f(t) = a_2 t^2 + a_3 t^3, \; 0 \leq t \leq T$$

$$f'(t) = 2a_2 t + 3a_3 t^2, \; 0 \leq t \leq T$$

Using these equations with the end conditions at $t = T$, we find:

$$f(T) = a_2 T^2 + a_3 T^3 = F$$

$$f'(T) = 2a_2 T + 3a_3 T^2 = 0$$

Solving these simultaneously for a_2 and a_3 yields:

$$a_2 = 3F/T^2$$
$$a_3 = -2F/T^3$$

Using these in the above equations yields the final form for our transitional braking force function:

$$f(t) = F[3(t/T)^2 - 2(t/T)^3], \; 0 \leq t \leq T$$

and its derivative

$$f'(t) = F[6(t/T) - 6(t/T)^2]/T, \ 0 \le t \le T$$

These polynomials can be checked by substituting the required end conditions.

Figure 3 plots the new brake force function and compares it to the straight-line approximation.

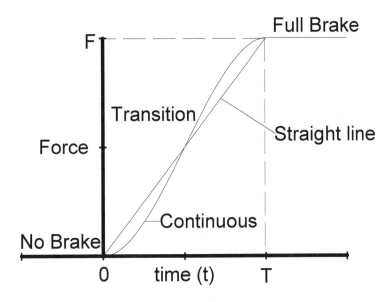

Figure 3. Comparison of continuous and straight-line braking force functions

Note the smoother transition from zero to full braking force - it appears to be a better physical model of the actual brake application process than the straight-line approximation. The continuous braking force function in Figure 3 is the one used to compute stopping distances for Boeing airplanes.

Problem 2 - Stopping Distance

Here, we combine the braking force function just developed with aerodynamic drag to find equations for computing stopping distance. This problem is a good example of procedures followed in solving real-world problems. The first equation comes from Newton's second law of motion:

$$\Sigma \text{ Forces} = \text{Mass} \times \text{Acceleration}$$

Mass is defined as weight (W) divided by the acceleration of gravity (g):

$$\text{Mass} = W/g$$

Acceleration is the first derivative of speed (S) with respect to time:

$$\text{Acceleration} = S'(t)$$

Recall brake force (f) is a function of time given by:

$$
\begin{aligned}
f(t) &= F[3(t/T)^2 - 2(t/T)^3], && 0 \le t \le T \\
&= F, && t > T
\end{aligned}
$$

The aerodynamic drag (d) is proportional to the square of the speed (based on Bernoulli's principle and conservation of momentum):

$$d(t) = kS^2(t)$$

The proportionality constant k depends primarily on air density and airplane shape. Substituting these two forces and the expressions for mass and acceleration into Newton's law, and solving for S'(t) yields:

$$S'(t) = -g[f(t) + d(t)]/W$$

Note both forces tend to decelerate (slow) the airplane so they have a negative sign.

How do we use this equation to find stopping distance? Note if we can integrate the S'(t) equation (find its anti-derivative), we know S as a function of time. And, S is the derivative of X (distance), or

$$X'(t) = S(t)$$

So, once we know S(t), we can find X(t) by finding the anti-derivative of the X'(t) equation. The complicated form for f(t) and the non-linearity in d(t) make finding the distance in a closed-form a formidable task. In fact, in the real stopping distance formulation (a far more complicated expression), it is impossible to solve directly for stopping distance. So, what do we do? We use a numerical approximation. This is the approach taken in nearly all real problems involving derivatives and anti-derivatives. The method used here is known as Euler integration and is the simplest way to solve such problems.

To use Euler integration, we define a small time step Δt and approximate the S(t) derivative by:

$$S'(t) \approx \frac{S(t+\Delta t) - S(t)}{\Delta t}$$

and the X(t) derivative by:

$$X'(t) \approx \frac{X(t+\Delta t) - X(t)}{\Delta t}$$

Note in both these approximations, if Δt goes to zero, we have the standard definition for a derivative. Solving for the values at $t + \Delta t$ yields

$$S(t + \Delta t) = S(t) + \Delta t S'(t)$$

$$X(t + \Delta t) = X(t) + \Delta t X'(t)$$

Assuming we know the current speed (S) and distance (X) at time t and the corresponding derivatives, these equations allow us to find the values of S and X at the next time value $t + \Delta t$. These become our new current values. Substituting these new values back into the above equations allows us to move ahead one more time step. By repeatedly using these equations, we can eventually find the stopping distance, the point where speed equals zero.

This process of Euler integration to compute stopping distance is best described as a series of steps:

1. Initialize t to zero, S to the speed of the airplane when stopping begins, and X to zero. Establish a value for Δt.

2. Compute braking force f(t) and aerodynamic drag d(t).

3. Compute S'(t) and X'(t).

4. Compute $S(t + \Delta t)$ and $X(t + \Delta t)$ using the previous formulae.

5. Check if $S(t + \Delta t)$ is less than or equal to zero. If so, airplane is stopped - time to stop is $t + \Delta t$ and distance to stop is $X(t + \Delta t)$. If not, set time to $t = t + \Delta t$, $S(t) = S(t + \Delta t)$, $X(t) = X(t + \Delta t)$ and return to step 2.

Let's look at such a table using the Boeing 777 airplane as an example.

Typical data for the 777 are:

Weight, W = 550,000 pounds

Full brake force, F = 100,000 pounds

Time to full brake, T = 10 seconds

Aerodynamic drag coefficient, k = 1.16

Initial speed, S(0) = 300 feet/second

and the acceleration of gravity is

$$g = 32.2 \; \frac{ft / sec}{sec}$$

One piece of critical information is still needed, the time step Δt. If we choose a Δt that is too large, accuracy will suffer because the derivative approximation is only valid for "small" Δt. But too small a Δt value will require many steps in the solution process. We need to choose a Δt that represents a reasonable compromise. The usual process is to choose a Δt that seems reasonable and compute a solution. Then, choose a smaller Δt and compute another solution. If the two solutions agree within acceptable bounds (we must, of course, define acceptable), we assume the solution is OK. Otherwise, a smaller Δt is needed. Table 1 on the next page shows sample computations (done with a calculator) for Δt = 2 seconds. We see from this table that it took between 42 and 44 seconds to stop the airplane and about 6309 feet of runway. These values can be narrowed down by interpolating the speed to an exact zero value. Doing so results in a stop time of 42.4 seconds in 6306.1 feet.

Table 1.

Sample Boeing 777 Stopping Distance Computations
(Formulas given at end of table)

Time t (s)	Speed S(t) (ft/sec)	Distance X(t) (ft)	Braking force f(t) (lb)	Drag d(t) (lb)	S'(t) (ft/sec^2)	X'(t) (ft/sec)	S(t+Δt) (ft/sec)	X(t+Δt) (ft)
0	300.00	0	0	104400	-6.112	300.00	287.78	600.0
2	287.78	600.0	10400	96068	-6.233	287.78	275.31	1175.6
4	275.31	1175.6	35200	87923	-7.208	275.31	260.89	1726.2
6	260.89	1726.2	64800	78954	-8.416	260.89	244.06	2248.0
8	244.06	2248.0	89600	69096	-9.291	244.06	225.48	2736.1
10	225.48	2736.1	100000	58976	-9.307	225.48	206.87	3187.1
12	206.87	3187.1	100000	49642	-8.761	206.87	189.35	3600.8
14	189.35	3600.8	100000	41590	-8.289	189.35	172.77	3979.5
16	172.77	3979.5	100000	34625	-7.882	172.77	157.01	4325.0
18	157.01	4325.0	100000	28596	-7.529	157.01	141.95	4639.0
20	141.95	4639.0	100000	23374	-7.223	141.95	127.50	4922.9
22	127.50	4922.9	100000	18857	-6.959	127.50	113.58	5177.9
24	113.58	5177.9	100000	14964	-6.731	113.58	100.12	5405.1
26	100.12	5405.1	100000	11628	-6.535	100.12	87.05	5605.3
28	87.05	5605.3	100000	8790	-6.369	87.05	74.31	5779.4
30	74.31	5779.4	100000	6405	-6.230	74.31	61.85	5928.0
32	61.85	5928.0	100000	4437	-6.114	61.85	49.62	6051.7
34	49.62	6051.7	100000	2856	-6.022	49.62	37.58	6150.9
36	37.58	6150.9	100000	1638	-5.950	37.58	25.68	6226.1
38	25.68	6226.1	100000	765	-5.899	25.68	13.88	6277.5
40	13.88	6277.5	100000	223	-5.868	13.88	2.14	6305.3
42	2.14	6305.3	100000	5	-5.855	2.14	-9.57	6309.6
44	-9.57	6309.6	100000	106	-5.861	-9.57	-21.29	6290.5

Formulae used to generate table columns:

Braking force, $f(t) = 100,000[3(t/10)^2 - 2(t/10)^3]$, $0 \le t \le 10$
$= 100,000$, $t > 10$

Drag, $d(t) = 1.16S(t)^2$
$S'(t) = -32.2[f(t) + d(t)]/550,000$
$X'(t) = S(t)$
$S(t + \Delta t) = S(t) + 2S'(t)$
$X(t + \Delta t) = X(t) + 2X'(t)$

Conclusions

We have looked at two problems involving derivatives to compute stopping distance for an airplane. We first developed a third-order polynomial description of braking force. This description was then used (with a model of aerodynamic drag) to solve two differential equations to find stopping distance and stopping time.

Additional questions for students include:

1. Discuss reasons for selecting a third-order polynomial to fit the brake force function. With a higher-order polynomial, what can be done with the superfluous coefficients? What other functions can be used for curve fitting?

2. Show that airplane speed is the same at $t = T$ for the straight-line approximation or the curve fit for brake force. Why use the curve fit?

3. Compare, using integration, the distance traveled while applying the brakes using the straight line and curve fit brake force functions. Is there a significant difference? You'll see the difference is minimal. So, why use the curve fit? The main reason is to insure the existence of a derivative at $t = 0$ and $t = T$. Many numerical solution techniques have performance problems when derivatives don't exist.

4. Develop a third-order polynomial that connects any two straight line segments, i.e. segments that don't necessarily have zero slopes.

5. Use a programming language (Visual Basic, for example) to code the numerical integration solution procedure. Use interpolation to find the zero-speed point. Our company, Kidware Software, offers several programming tutorials (Visual Basic, Small Basic, Visual C#, Java) that provide the skills to build such a program – see our website http://www.kidwaresoftware.com for details.

6. Study the sensitivity of stopping distance to the solution time step Δt. How large can Δt be without sacrificing accuracy? How is program (or solution) execution time affected by very small Δt values?

7. Compare stopping performance of various airplanes. For example, typical numbers for Boeing aircraft are:

Model	Weight (lb)	Full brake force (lb)	Time to full brake	Drag constant k	Initial speed (ft/sec)
737	300,000	40,000	8	1.05	300
747	700,000	120,000	15	1.20	300
757	400,000	45,000	10	1.10	300
767	500,000	100,000	10	1.15	300
777	550,000	100,000	10	1.16	300

8. Investigate and discuss the physical reasonability of the braking force and aerodynamic drag models. How would the model coefficients change for more powerful brakes, for wet brakes, for no brakes, or for a sleeker, more aerodynamic airplane?

9. How would you modify the stopping distance equations to include reverse thrust? Similar to aerodynamic drag, thrust is directly proportional to the speed squared. A simple way to account for this thrust is to just adjust the k factor in aerodynamic drag. Would you decrease or increase k to include reverse thrust?

10. Note the aerodynamic drag (as modeled here) is always positive. This gives an incorrect value when S becomes negative, because drag, like friction, must oppose motion. This is no problem here because we stop solving the problem when S is zero. Many systems with friction have both positive and negative

182

speeds. One example is an oscillating pendulum. Develop a friction model that is proportional to speed-squared that always opposes motion.

11. Use the numerical integration method to solve other problems involving derivatives, for example for vehicle speed, economic growth rates, population dynamics, home heating, rocket dynamics, or pendulum dynamics.

Appendix: STEM Simulation Software Ideas

Several times throughout Real-World STEM we have suggested writing a computer program to simulate the STEM problems we have been reviwing using a computer application. Below are some screenshots to several of the Real-World STEM applications we have developed. We originally wrote these STEM applications using Microsoft Visual Basic and we are now in the process of porting them to Microsoft Windows 10 using Microsoft Visual C#. If you are interested in learning how to write your own STEM Simulation software please check out our various computer programming tutorials at our website: https://www.kidwaresoftware.com.

Levers: Levers teaches you about the three different lever types and forces required to balance them.

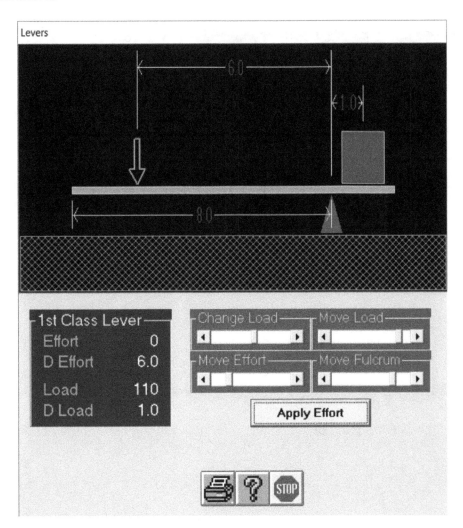

Pendulum: Study basic oscillations with Pendulum -- see effects of changing lengths, weight, and friction. Plots of motion are given.

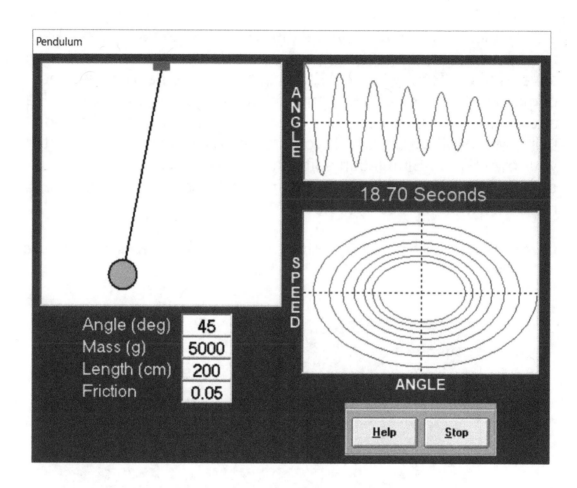

Water Wheel demonstrates the exciting world of chaotic dynamics. Examine wheel motion as different water flow rates are used.

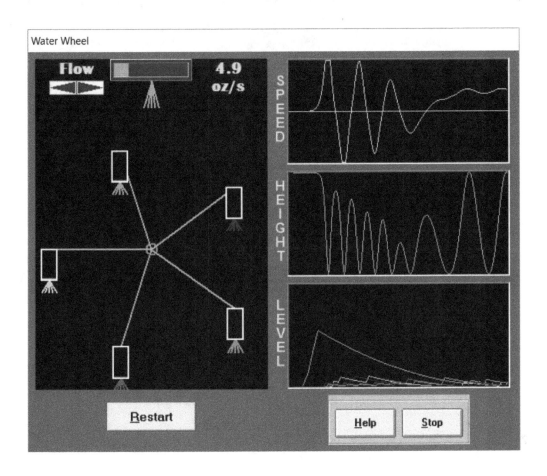

Moon Lander gives practice in understanding concepts of speed and acceleration as you try to land on the moon.

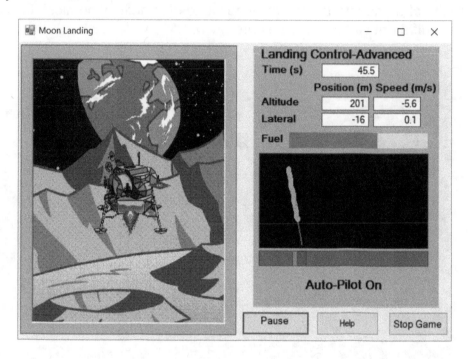

Weather Watch provides tools that allow you to identify and predict trends in the weather.

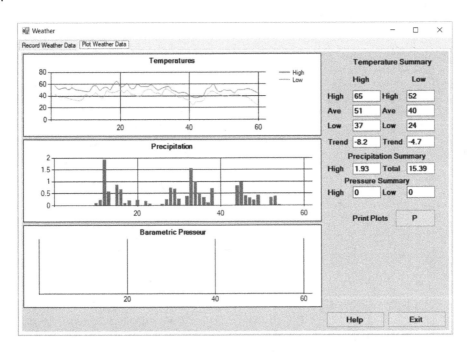

Circuits allows you to build electric circuits from batteries, switches, and light bulbs. See effects of different circuit types, burned out bulbs, etc.

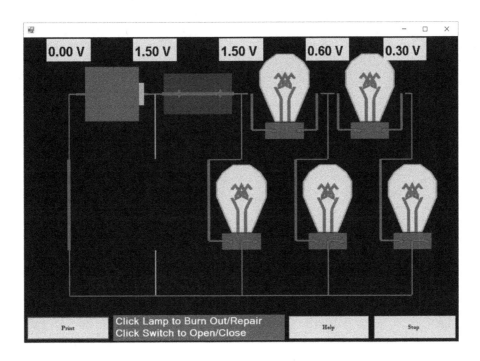

Robotics allows you to study the world of robots using a 2-dimensional, two-link robotic arm. Trajectories is a simulation of a flying object. The program introduces estimation and answer refinement skills.

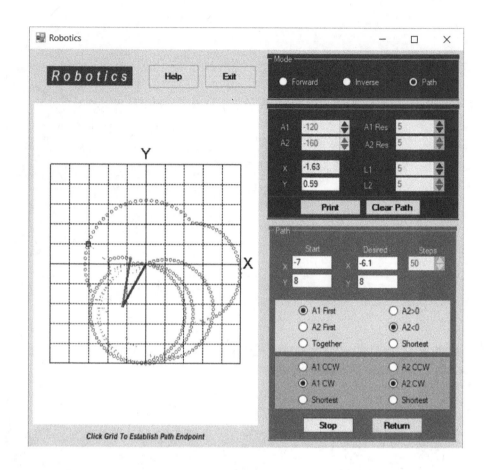

Rocketry is a demonstration of model rocket launches - vary thrust, burn time, and rocket mass.

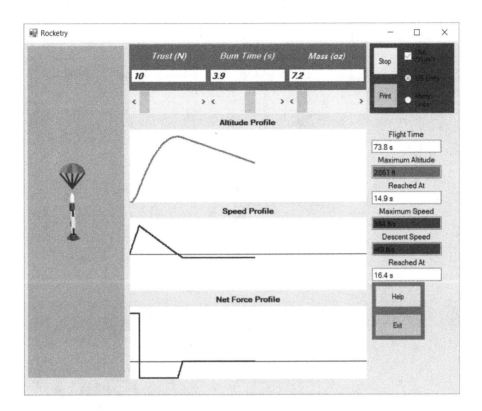

Probability introduces an exciting field of mathematics with problems in coin flipping, dice rolling, and dropping toothpicks!

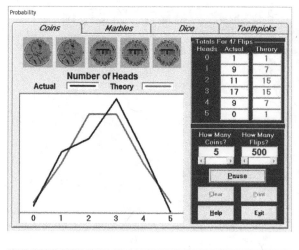

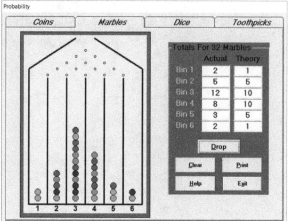

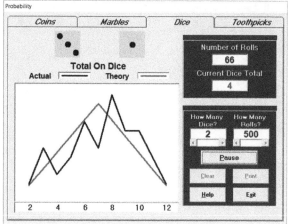

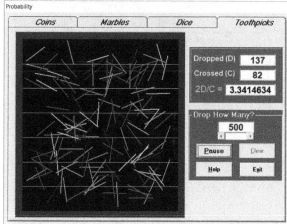

Trajectores is used to discover the basics of ballistics, or motion in the X-Y plane. The application has no right or wrong answers -- it simply provides an arena for trying different things and seeing the results.

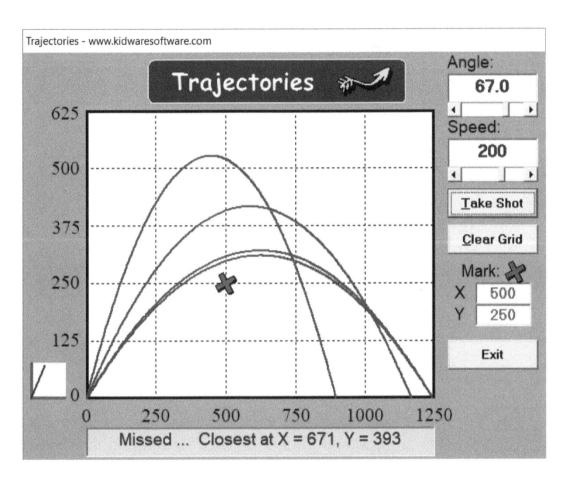

The general idea of the program is to determine at what angle (measured from the horizontal, or X, axis) and speed an object should be launched (starting at X=0, Y=0) to hit a specific point. The object moves in the X-Y plane (Y=0 representing the ground) under the influence of gravity in the negative y-direction, i.e. the object will fall down. The X-Y plane and concept of an angle should be explained to the user, at a level the user can understand. With this general basis, several exercises can be tried.

Once the program begins, the X-Y grid is drawn and several options presented. On the screen is a crossmark that represents the point you want to hit. That mark's X and Y location are given on the right side of the screen. This mark is moved by simply dragging it (using the mouse) to the desired position. The object angle is changed using the scroll bar under Angle. Clicking the end arrows changes the angle by 0.1 degree, while clicking the bar area changes the angle by 1 degree. The angle value (ranging from 0 to 90 degrees) is shown above this scroll bar and a small grid in the lower left corner graphically indicates current object angle. The object speed (ranging from 0 to 300) is changed with scroll bar under Speed. Clicking the end arrows changes the speed by 1, while clicking the bar area changes the speed by 10.   Once you have the mark where you want it and have the angle and speed at desired values, you take a shot by clicking 'Take Shot'.

A plot of the object's trajectory is drawn and you are told whether or not you hit your desired mark. If you missed, you are told how close you came. At this point, you can change the object angle, speed, or even move your mark and take more shots. The subsequent shots are plotted on the screen. To clear the plot(s) at any time, click Clear Grid. The program is stopped at any time by clicking 'Exit'.

Polynomial Fractals draws fractals based on the solution of polynomials. The theory behind the program is described in our tutorial "Fractals from Polynomial Solutions", available from our website.

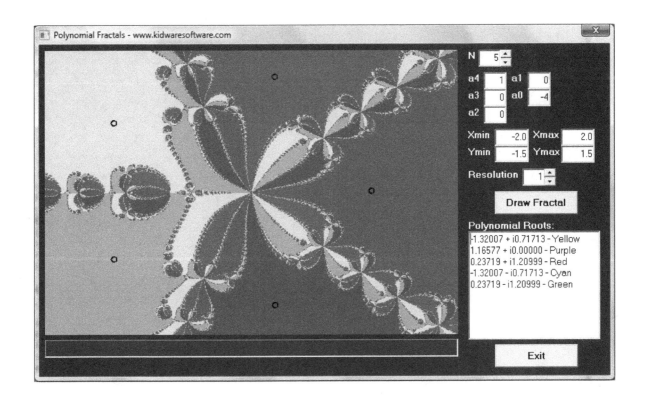

In this program, you set the order of the polynomial (n) you want to solve (2 through 9). Then, you enter values for each ai coefficient (i=0, ..., n-1). You establish values for xmin, xmax, ymin and ymax. Lastly, you set a resolution value (1 through 10). This establishes the size of the 'dot' used to represent an initial root guess. For a resolution of 1, every dot in the fractal display area (over 240,000 points) will be individually colored. This results in a pretty plot, but takes some time. Play around with different resolution values. In the code, onvergence checks are made with a value of e = 0.000001. Iterations are limited to a maximum of 1000 to avoid infinite loops.

Once all values are set, you click the 'Draw Fractal' button. As each root is found, it is listed, along with the color used to represent it. A progress bar indicates how much time remains to see the fractal. The program takes a while to run - at times, it may seem like it's actually stopped (especially for low resolution values). Be patient, the fractals will appear!

Also, there is some error checking in the program, but it does assume you enter proper numbers where required.

OUR ORACLE JAVA PROGRAMMING TUTORIALS

Java™ For Kids is a beginning programming tutorial consisting of 10 chapters explaining (in simple, easy-to-follow terms) how to build a Java application. Students learn about project design, object-oriented programming, console applications, graphics applications and many elements of the Java language. Numerous examples are used to demonstrate every step in the building process. The projects include a number guessing game, a card game, an allowance calculator, a state capitals game, Tic-Tac-Toe, a simple drawing program, and even a basic video game. Designed for kids ages 12 and up.

Beginning Java™ is a semester long "beginning" programming tutorial consisting of 10 chapters explaining (in simple, easy-to-follow terms) how to build a Java application. The tutorial includes several detailed computer projects for students to build and try. These projects include a number guessing game, card game, allowance calculator, drawing program, state capitals game, and a couple of video games like Pong. We also include several college prep bonus projects including a loan calculator, portfolio manager, and checkbook balancer. Designed for students age 15 and up.

Learn Java™ GUI Applications is a 9 lesson Tutorial covering object-oriented programming concepts, using an integrated development environment to create and test Java projects, building and distributing GUI applications, understanding and using the Swing control library, exception handling, sequential file access, graphics, multimedia, advanced topics such as printing, and help system authoring. Our Beginning Java or Java For Kids tutorial is a pre-requisite for this tutorial

Programming Games with Java™ is a semester long "intermediate" programming tutorial consisting of 10 chapters explaining (in simple, easy-to-follow terms) how to build a Visual C# Video Games. The games built are non-violent, family-friendly and teach logical thinking skills. Students will learn how to program the following Visual C# video games: Safecracker, Tic Tac Toe, Match Game, Pizza Delivery, and Moon Landing. This intermediate level self-paced tutorial can be used at home or school. The tutorial is simple enough for kids yet engaging enough for beginning adults. Our Learn Java GUI Applications tutorial is a required pre-requisite for this tutorial.

Java™ Homework Projects is a Java GUI Swing tutorial covering object-oriented programming concepts. It explains (in simple, easy-to-follow terms) how to build Java GUI project to use around the home. Students learn about project design, the Java Swing controls, many elements of the Java language, and how to distribute finished projects. The projects built include a Dual-Mode Stopwatch, Flash Card Math Quiz, Multiple Choice Exam, Blackjack Card Game, Weight Monitor, Home Inventory Manager and a Snowball Toss Game. Our Learn Java GUI Applications tutorial is a pre-requisite for this tutorial

OUR MICROSOFT SMALL BASIC PROGRAMMING TUTORIALS

Small Basic For Kids is an illustrated introduction to computer programming that provides an interactive, self-paced tutorial to the new Small Basic programming environment. The book consists of 30 short lessons that explain how to create and run a Small Basic program. Elementary students learn about program design and many elements of the Small Basic language. Numerous examples are used to demonstrate every step in the building process. The tutorial also includes two complete games (Hangman and Pizza Zapper) for students to build and try. Designed for kids ages 8+.

The Beginning Microsoft Small Basic Programming Tutorial is a self-study first semester "beginner" programming tutorial consisting of 11 chapters explaining (in simple, easy-to-follow terms) how to write Microsoft Small Basic programs. Numerous examples are used to demonstrate every step in the building process. The last chapter of this tutorial shows you how four different Small Basic games could port to Visual Basic, Visual C# and Java. This beginning level self-paced tutorial can be used at home or at school. The tutorial is simple enough for kids ages 10+ yet engaging enough for adults.

Basic Computer Games - Small Basic Edition is a re-make of the classic BASIC COMPUTER GAMES book originally edited by David H. Ahl. It contains 100 of the original text based BASIC games that inspired a whole generation of programmers. Now these classic BASIC games have been re-written in Microsoft Small Basic for a new generation to enjoy! The new Small Basic games look and act like the original text based games. The book includes all the original spaghetti code and GOTO commands!

Programming Home Projects with Microsoft Small Basic is a self-paced programming tutorial explains (in simple, easy-to-follow terms) how to build Small Basic Windows applications. Students learn about program design, Small Basic objects, many elements of the Small Basic language, and how to debug and distribute finished programs. Sequential file input and output is also introduced. The projects built include a Dual-Mode Stopwatch, Flash Card Math Quiz, Multiple Choice Exam, Blackjack Card Game, Weight Monitor, Home Inventory Manager and a Snowball Toss Game.

The Developer's Reference Guide to Microsoft Small Basic While developing all the different Microsoft Small Basic tutorials we found it necessary to write The Developer's Reference Guide to Microsoft Small Basic. The Developer's Reference Guide to Microsoft Small Basic is over 500 pages long and includes over 100 Small Basic programming examples for you to learn from and include in your own Microsoft Small Basic programs. It is a detailed reference guide for new developers.

David Ahl's Small Basic Computer Adventures is a Microsoft Small Basic re-make of the classic *Basic Computer Games* programming *book* originally written by David H. Ahl. This new book includes the following classic adventure simulations; Marco Polo, Westward Ho!, The Longest Automobile Race, The Orient Express, Amelia Earhart: Around the World Flight, Tour de France, Subway Scavenger, Hong Kong Hustle, and Voyage to Neptune. Learn how to program these classic computer simulations in Microsoft Small Basic.

OUR MICROSOFT VISUAL BASIC PROGRAMMING TUTORIALS

Beginning Visual Basic® is a semester long self-paced "beginner" programming tutorial consisting of 10 chapters explaining (in simple, easy-to-follow terms) how to build a Visual Basic Windows application. The tutorial includes several detailed computer projects for students to build and try. These projects include a number guessing game, card game, allowance calculator, drawing program, state capitals game, and a couple of video games like Pong. We also include several college prep bonus projects including a loan calculator, portfolio manager, and checkbook balancer. Designed for students age 15 and up.

LEARN VISUAL BASIC is a comprehensive college level programming tutorial covering object-oriented programming, the Visual Basic integrated development environment, building and distributing Windows applications using the Windows Installer, exception handling, sequential file access, graphics, multimedia, advanced topics such as web access, printing, and HTML help system authoring. The tutorial also introduces database applications (using ADO .NET) and web applications (using ASP.NET).

VISUAL BASIC AND DATABASES is a tutorial that provides a detailed introduction to using Visual Basic for accessing and maintaining databases for desktop applications. Topics covered include: database structure, database design, Visual Basic project building, ADO .NET data objects (connection, data adapter, command, data table), data bound controls, proper interface design, structured query language (SQL), creating databases using Access, SQL Server and ADOX, and database reports. Actual projects developed include a book tracking system, a sales invoicing program, a home inventory system and a daily weather monitor.

199

OUR MICROSOFT VISUAL C# PROGRAMMING TUTORIALS

Beginning Visual C#® is a semester long "beginning" programming tutorial consisting of 10 chapters explaining (in simple, easy-to-follow terms) how to build a C# Windows application. The tutorial includes several detailed computer projects for students to build and try. These projects include a number guessing game, card game, allowance calculator, drawing program, state capitals game, and a couple of video games like Pong.   We also include several college prep bonus projects including a loan calculator, portfolio manager, and checkbook balancer. Designed for students ages 15+.

LEARN VISUAL C# is a comprehensive college level computer programming tutorial covering object-oriented programming, the Visual C# integrated development environment and toolbox, building and distributing Windows applications (using the Windows Installer), exception handling, sequential file input and output, graphics, multimedia effects (animation and sounds), advanced topics such as web access, printing, and HTML help system authoring. The tutorial also introduces database applications (using ADO .NET) and web applications (using ASP.NET).

VISUAL C# AND DATABASES is a tutorial that provides a detailed introduction to using Visual C# for accessing and maintaining databases for desktop applications. Topics covered include: database structure, database design, Visual C# project building, ADO .NET data objects (connection, data adapter, command, data table), data bound controls, proper interface design, structured query language (SQL), creating databases using Access, SQL Server and ADOX, and database reports. Actual projects developed include a book tracking system, a sales invoicing program, a home inventory system and a daily weather monitor.

www.ingramcontent.com/pod-product-compliance
Lightning Source LLC
LaVergne TN
LVHW060140070326
832902LV00018B/2878